The Spiritual Legacy Journey

The Spiritual Legacy Journey
Create a Spiritual Legacy for Your Family

Lois L. Mayo, PhD

A DIVISION OF
LIBERTY UNIVERSITY

ISBN 13: 978-1-935986-83-6

Contact the author at: llmayo@liberty.edu

Liberty University Press
Lynchburg, VA

For Luke, Allie, and Julia

Contents

How to Start Your Journey 1

1. My Mom: Mission and Celebration 9

2. My Dad: Faith and Reading 21

3. My Grandma Wagner: Home and Rejoice 29

4. My Grandma Campbell: Simplicity and Love 36

5. My Sister, Holly: Discipline and Adventure 45

6. My Brother, Chuck: Work and Visit 56

7. My Sister, Becky: Friendliness and Giving 61

8. My Friend, Jennifer: Kindness and Friendship 68

9. My Neighbor, Ann: Neighbors and Choice 76

10. Luke and Lois: Prayer and Fruit of the Spirit 82

11. A Year Later 86

Conclusion 98

How to Start Your Journey

Proverbs 1:8-9 states, "Hear, my son, your father's instruction, and forsake not your mother's teaching, for they are a graceful garland for your head and pendants for your neck" (ESV). What kind of garland and pendants am I placing on my children?

Becoming a parent is amazing, scary, and humbling. At some point after the baby showers, the labor and delivery, and adjusting to your new life, you find yourself thinking about this awesome responsibility of raising children. You see them learning and growing, their little faces intent on yours, and you can sense the power you possess to influence them. But life is busy, and making it through each day, making it through the work week, getting the house passably clean, children fed in a reasonably healthy fashion, keeping the house standing…well, the list goes on and on…it is easy to float along. Which brings to mind, perhaps the most common cliché wistfully expressed by parents everywhere…it goes by so fast, before you know it they'll be in school, college, having kids of their own. Having heard this countless times, and having seen the last few years fly by with my own two girls, while at the same time, slowly making my way through the work week so that I can reach the weekend and spend more time at home, I have to believe this must be true; it will all go by in a blink of the eye.

I have two main concerns about this unreasonable passage of time. The first is that I want to actively teach my children a few things before it's too late. My second concern is that my memory will fade over time. I read about a study where women were asked if they had breastfed their babies or used formula, and the majority of women remembered incorrectly. They answered based on the current, popular trend. (Apparently, they had some kind of records to show if they had truly breastfed or used formula.) Now, I find it incredible that any woman could forget this, but it seems poor autobiographical memory is pretty well documented. People even go to school to study it. I distinctly recall breastfeeding both my children. But out of respect for the scholarly literature out there, I concede that I may forget a lot of things I want to share with my girls as the time goes by.

Sure, I could hope that I will subconsciously teach my girls, that I will slip in a few wise maxims here and there over grocery shopping and hitting the playgrounds, but I don't trust myself or this mysterious, rapid speed vs. parenting conflict. What if we as parents, took the time to actually choose what it is we want to pass on to our children, thought about what is important to us, put it down on paper, and passed it on? Would we be able to relax some day with guilt-free consciences, knowing that we had done our best with the time we had for our children? I know that a clean house is only so important, but it is easy to immediately see the results when I vacuum up cracker crumbs. Passing on wisdom is more important to me, so shouldn't I do something concrete such as write it down, make a specific plan, and look for the results? Second Timothy 3:1-5 contains this warning,

> But understand this, that in the last days there will come times of difficulty. For people will be lovers of self, lovers of money, proud, arrogant, abusive, disobedient to their parents, ungrateful, unholy, heartless, unappeasable, slanderous, without self-control, brutal, not loving good, treacherous, reckless, swollen with conceit, lovers of pleasure rather than lovers of God, having the appearance of godliness, but denying its power. Avoid such people. (ESV)

I have to admit, if this was a list of heinous crimes with things like murder and kidnapping on it, I might not pay as close attention, but if you read over the list again, you'll see these are more subtle attributes. These negative character traits are all around us. I certainly do not want my precious children to be taught by these examples, so what do I want to teach them?

We as parents need to take the bull by the horns. I am not going to worry so much about the house (I'll still obsess a little bit). I am going to make a formal plan for passing on wisdom to my children, before I forget and the chance slips by. We all make mistakes as parents, so we should probably take the opportunity to prepare ourselves, by creating and outlining our parenting goals; and who knows, it just might make a difference. It is my hope that the journaling example I provide in this book will inspire you to write your own parenting journal, one that specifies the spiritual legacies you want to live in your life, and pass onto your children.

For years the culture has graciously allowed us to blame our parents to the point of it becoming a joke. I am old enough to know better. I suspect we all have aspects of our childhood we would change if we could. (Personally, I am content to see to it that particularly bad photos are destroyed.) Ephesians 6:2 commands us to honor our parents, and I am pretty sure a play-by-play of all the bad parenting moments we may have experienced doesn't come under the heading of honoring mom and dad. We can choose what we want to focus on and think about, and definitely what we want to make a point of passing on to our children. After all, how is dwelling on negative events or situations going to make me or my children better people? Philippians 4:8 advises, "Finally brothers and sisters, whatever is true, whatever is noble, whatever is right, whatever is pure, whatever is lovely, whatever is admirable—if anything is excellent or praiseworthy—think about such things" (NIV). So, first I will choose to remember and share positive things about my past.

When I concentrate on what I want to be sure to share with my children, my mind starts to wander through the people in my childhood. I could be wrong, but I think the people in our lives shape who we become, if not entirely, than at least more than circumstances. My first goal during this journey is to be positive; my second goal is to identify the legacies of people in my life that I want to use to continue to shape my life and to pass on to my children. After I have explored my childhood family and friends' legacies, I hope to have a better grasp on the legacy my husband and I want to leave our children. Legacy is a weighty word. I don't know how much money I'll have to leave, and if our current financial portfolio (and I use the word portfolio loosely here) is any indication, I should probably focus on non-fiscal legacies for my children.

When I was a young girl I read a series of books by Arleta Richardson, called *In Grandma's Attic*, *More Stories from Grandma's Attic*, and *Still More Stories from Grandma's Attic*. I loved reading about the life lessons this grandma shared with her granddaughter, along with the tidbits about growing up in a different era, things like hoop skirts, buggy rides, and pumping water. I don't know if my children will be amused by my old friendship beads, VCRs, and a daredevil childhood without a bike helmet, but I like the idea of sharing how things were different, and of course, those things that don't change, like the beauty of time spent together in the kitchen, and the wonder of holidays shared.

I don't want to bore you with my personal legacies, so I hope you will share the journey with me and think about your own childhoods, the legacies within, and start to outline the wisdom you want to leave your children, as well as the wisdom you want to choose to live by. Perhaps this book can be a road map for you to follow in finding your own legacies. Below is a chart outlining the process of creating a parenting journal (which I model in this book).

Five Steps	Explanation	Example
Name and Relationship	Make a list of the people in your life who have influenced who you are today. Do this quickly, without much thought, and chances are, the first people that come to mind make up the list you are looking for. You can see the list I came up with in the table of contents.	My Mom
Memories associated with this person and legacy	Put your memories in writing. What would be fun and special to share with your family about this person? When you think of this person, what stories come to mind? What do you most admire about this person? There are some memories that in the moment we know are going to stay with us forever. These are the memories to pass on to our loved ones. Focus on positive memories.	The first memories that came to my mind were about meals. Then, I thought of ways my mom took care of me and others, which high-lighted her mission in life.

Legacy in one word	Identify one or two qualities from your memories that you have learned from each person that you want to live out and pass on to your children. Try to narrow each quality or legacy down to one word.	Mission (For me, the word "mission" represents my mother's legacy to me, because I see her having a mission in life, and excelling at it.)
Legacy commitment: Statement of the legacy you see in this person. Statement of how you will fulfill this legacy. Statement of how you will raise your children to fulfill this legacy.	Now it is time to make a legacy commitment. First, explain the legacy in a sentence. Next, state what you will do in your life to display this legacy. Then, state what you will do to help your children learn this legacy.	I respect my mother for nursing sick and dying people. I admire her for finding something she is good at and using it to help many people throughout her life. I choose to learn from her, and begin to identify my gift and how I can use it to help people. I will closely watch my children, look for their gifts and talents, and encourage them to identify their gifts and use them to help others.
Legacy scripture verses to commit to memory	Find Scripture verses to commit to memory that give significance to the legacy	Jeremiah 29:11, Romans 8:26-31, Psalm 139:13

The Spiritual Legacy Journey begins with identifying the individuals in your childhood who have impacted who you are today. For me, this was my parents, two grandmothers, three siblings, childhood friend, and a neighbor. When I think about my childhood, these are the people I most want my children to know about. The exact number of people that you choose for your journey will vary depending on your situation. You might have other relatives, school or church teachers, or multiple friends you want to include. Personally, I limited this selection to my childhood, though I am sure that we continue to be impacted by those we come into contact with throughout our lives. I focused on my childhood because I wanted to share it with my children, and because it lays the foundation for who I am today. (Starting this part of the journey also makes you pause to think about who you might be impacting right now, in addition to your own children.)

Once you have chosen the individuals you want to include in your journal, the next step is to start thinking, reminiscing, and writing it all down. I did not talk with others I know about their memories during this step, because I wanted it to be about what I remember. The goal in this first section is to document memories of each person that you want to pass onto your children because they are important memories you think your children will enjoy hearing about. This is particularly fun when faced with changing technology and times, like when I explain to my children that we had to rent a huge VCR from the video store for the weekend to watch movies. As a mom, I chose to start with my mother, then my grandmothers, followed by my siblings in birth order, then my best friend, and finally my neighbor. You can choose to put individuals in order by age, how they impacted you, when you met them, or randomly.

No doubt, one of the biggest challenges in taking this journey, are negative memories. I did not include any negative memories in my journal because that is not what this journey was about for me. I choose to focus on the positive in my life, and while I have every reason to, I am not naively suggesting that all childhood memories are rosy and perfect. An important aspect of this journey is choice. In thinking about the individuals from my childhood, and the legacies I want to leave my children, it occurred to me that I choose what to grasp and learn from the character of each person. I did not create false memories or try to gloss over imperfections, and I do not recommend you do either. It is essential to carefully consider each person you want to include in your journey. If there are individuals from your childhood who cause painful and negative memories for you, it may not be beneficial to include them when you think about leaving spiritual legacies to your children. Be honest with yourself when you evaluate this, because this is an opportunity to recognize the good qualities in others that you can choose to instill in your character and to pass onto your children.

I included random memories that came to my mind. For example, when I talk about my mom, I included the foods we liked to eat. For my dad, I included books we read that are important for me to pass on to my children. You will no doubt, go down any number of different trails with your memories. There is no definite list of items you need to include, but my journey may serve up some suggestions for you. During this exploration I decided to conclude with two legacies per person because I found it difficult to narrow it down to one (especially because I started with those closest to me). There is no rule that says you need two per person, or even the same number per person in your journey. I like things neat and organized, so for my brain, two per person worked best.

I also found it helpful to try to condense these legacies to one word each. Originally, I had a statement for each, but found I wasn't able to recall much as the legacies piled up. I found it more meaningful to put the memory into one word per legacy.

Once the legacies have been decided upon, it is time to further define them in the context of your memories for that person. Put in writing the memories it is important for you to share with your family, focusing on stories that highlight the legacies you have selected. Next, make a legacy commitment with a summarizing statement, followed by how you will live this spiritual legacy, and then a statement of how you will pass this legacy onto your children. I see this journal as a first step in the journey of spiritual legacies. At first, these commitment statements will be basic and general, but over time, you can go back and add more specific items that you have discovered will instill these legacies in your life and in your children's lives.

After completing my legacy commitments and selecting specific memories, the process of making these statements made me think about various related concerns or topics I also wanted to pass onto my children. For this purpose, I created a category for each person called "Thinking About Our Legacies." For example, when I wrote about my mom, I could not help but think about women's roles in the home. When I wrote about my sister's sense of adventure, I found myself making a crazy list of all the places I want to visit with my family.

I ended up with 20 legacies, which I will not deny is a lot. Throughout the process I relied on the Bible to help me understand each legacy and define how I wanted to live it out. I feel very strongly that Scripture memorization is an excellent tool for Christian living. I selected verses to memorize for each person to help me begin to live out their legacy. The Bible is my authority, so it was important for me to base the legacies on God's Word to enforce their significance and better allow me to remember each one. This reminds me that God has always been working in my life.

I always wanted to keep one of those mother's journals where you record your children's milestones and your hopes and prayers for them. Every time I started a journal, I neglected it just a few short weeks or months later. In creating this journaling process, I found myself for the first time able to complete a journal I will be pleased to share with my children someday. I was motivated by how quickly my girls were growing. My oldest daughter lost her first baby tooth the other day, and yes, my eyes watered a bit. I am scared I will miss my opportunity to pass on the important things in life, and I did not even know what it was I wanted to share with them before I sat down and organized my thoughts in this journal.

My hope is that you too will be able to complete this journal and find it helpful and meaningful when starting to think about what it is you have learned and what you want to pass onto your children. There are no deadlines or rules. By creating a model for your spiritual legacy journey, my goal was to take some of the work out of the process, and make it fun, enjoyable, and instructional.

Of course, you do not have to be married or have children to begin the spiritual legacy journey. I think this journey is best begun as soon as possible, as soon as one starts thinking about identity, character, and purpose. An engaged couple could complete this journal together and share their background with each other, and plan their spiritual legacies together.

Single adults have just as much reason to take a spiritual legacy journey as anyone else. Define who you are, or others will do so for you. Think about who you are influencing, and who you might want to impact. Ultimately, we answer to God, but He has created us as relational people, and expects us to reach out to one another.

Chapter 1

My Mom: Mission and Celebration

It was natural for me to start with my mom, but I recommend you begin where you think it makes the most sense for you. It was kind of a revelation for me that my mom had a calling in nursing that she followed. It turned out that having a mission in life was a great place to start my journey. One of my favorite things about my mom is her sense of celebration which I happily pass on to my children. As you read my example, I hope it will jog your memories and give you ideas for beginning your journey.

Moms and food kind of go together. I don't know if my children will be interested, but I am going to meander down Memory Lane on the subject of all things food. For all my complaining about dinner growing up, I had no idea just how difficult it can be to put together a healthy, balanced meal every day. Add in the rush to get a meal on the table after working all day, plus finicky, ever-changing toddler preferences and you really have a challenge on your hands. We ate canned vegetables growing up, and as an adult I was shocked to find out how tasty fresh or frozen peas are. They don't taste anything like the canned kind. I don't think spinach was ever meant to be canned. We did have corn on the cob a lot, though in the winter we resorted back to creamed corn. My mom made spaghetti, meatloaf, and lemon pepper chicken. I remember these strange turkey croquets my sister, Holly, especially liked. I'm not sure what they were stuffed with, maybe some kind of rice concoction. Holly also liked peanut butter toast, and my mom likes to remind her occasionally of the time she tried toasting the bread with the peanut butter already spread on it. Afterward, we had a large black spot under the cupboard from where the fire was put out. It's probably still there.

My mom would make us sit at the table until we finished our meal, and I often had to sit there a long time. Basically, I was waiting for everyone to leave the area so I could come up with creative ways to dispose of the offending Brussel sprouts or other off-green mushy vegetable. It wasn't her fault, because when I talk to other people my age, they express the same uncertainty as to why all vegetables were cooked as long as possible, until there was no crunch or life left in them, and they had undergone several color changes. My children will probably complain that I undercooked our fresh vegetables. For a reason unknown to us children, there was a small, quarter-sized hole in our dining room floor. It was not uncommon for us to drop an unsavory morsel or two down the little hole during desperate meal times. We didn't know where the food went to because we never saw the remnants in the cellar. Of course, the dog was always an obvious savior, but you had to be quick about it, as our mom was on to that trick. I particularly recall sitting at the table for long periods of time when soup was on the menu. My mom would throw all kinds of leftovers into soup. There was no recipe, and no rules. I have never liked to see my food all mixed up in a way that camouflages the individual ingredients. Soup was scary, hard to slip down into the hole in the floor, and impossible to hand off to the dog. The worst case scenario was when my mom would release me from table duty only to put the plate or bowl in the refrigerator until later. It felt like the worst kind of torture.

We went through one pleasant time period where we had a deep fryer coated in Crisco that we would pull out of the refrigerator a few times a week. My friend, Jeni, and I would throw in curly fries and chicken nuggets. We were also famous for making Kraft macaroni and cheese on a fairly regular basis. We came up with some fun treats that we regularly visited, such as pound cake with chocolate peanut butter ice cream, or ice cream with popcorn on it. We made air popcorn and coated it in melted butter. We weren't that excited when microwave popcorn came out because it was never the same. We always had a huge stash of Kool-Aid packets ready to go. Funny thing is we didn't think anything of mixing in all that sugar and pouring a glass of blue, lip-smacking, vaguely berry flavored Kool-Aid.

The only meal I recall my dad making, other than grilling, is pancakes.

He loves pancakes. This was a special treat, along with the donuts he would bring home sometimes. He loves donuts too. He would buy a box of plain, white and cinnamon powdered donuts. I distinctly recall my Grandma Campbell licking the tip of her finger and tapping it on the table against all those little escaping powder crumbs.

For all the mushy vegetables and mystery soups, my mother more than made up for it in desserts like pecan pie, Texas sheet cake, and every kind of cookie out there. I used to love it when she would make a pie, because she would make little jam tarts for me with the left over dough.

Once in a great while we could buy lunch at school. Of course we saved this treat for the square pizza you pealed out of plastic, or turkey on a stick which came with an ice cream scoop-shaped ball of rice. I have an extreme aversion to meat on a stick to this day, and I try to avoid fairs or festivals where this is considered a specialty of the event. My mom insisted on buying this bologna with olive pieces in it that I simply detested. I can't for the life of me figure out why she bought it when no one ever ate it. The only thing I can think of is that maybe it was really inexpensive. It didn't matter because she also bought pies, four for a dollar, that were coated in a smooth sugar icing. Fruit rollups became a big hit when I was in elementary school, but I honestly didn't like the taste of chewy jelly.

Mission

When I think of my mother, after I stop thinking about food, I think of my mom taking care of people for a living. I guess that's the most important thing to know about her. I believe everyone has a gift to share with others, and nursing is my mom's gift. It takes a special person to provide hospice care and watch over a dying friend, as all of my mom's patients eventually become friends.

My mom has provided hospice care to countless people in her life. Sometimes, they would live with us, which I have to admit, I didn't always like, other than when my Grandma Lucille Wagner lived with us when she couldn't live alone anymore. For someone who takes care of people for a living, bringing Grandma to live with us was the obvious thing to do, and I liked having her with us. I was in high school at the time, and I respected my mom for welcoming Grandma into our home.

My mom worked in a hospital for years. One of my favorite Halloween memories was when my best friend, Jeni, wore my mom's white
nursing uniform, a now long-gone tradition. My mom bandaged me up
from head to toe, and Jeni and I went trick-or-treating together, with me
hobbling on crutches.

I remember when I had my wisdom teeth taken out, and my mom
cared for me for a whole week. She made these special orange milkshakes
that were delicious. I had already graduated from college and was living
in Palmyra, PA. I went back to Binghamton, NY to have my wisdom
teeth taken out, and my mom was happy to take care of me, or at least
it seemed that way to me. In a strange sort of way, I actually enjoyed
that time together.

There are lots of ways to help people for a living, some more obvious
than others. Discover what your life's goal is, and when it is directed
toward helping others, your pursuit of that goal will be more steadfast.

My mom was always the first to bring a meal to a family with someone
ill or recovering from a hospital visit. She always went to calling hours
and funerals to pay her respects. My mom went to all the baby and
bridal showers and weddings she was invited to, almost like it was her
duty to the new mom, bride or groom, and often because she knew their
parents. It's a sign of respect to go to things you are invited to, whether
you want to or not. It is also a good reminder to take the time and effort
to celebrate the joys in others' lives too.

Celebration

Here's another thing I always loved about my mom, and something I
hope I learned from her. My mom celebrates the holidays in a big way. We
always had decorations in the windows for Halloween, Easter, Valentine's
Day, and of course, Christmas. At Christmas we'd spray fake snow on the
windows, and put candles on each window sill. You couldn't put out too
many decorations. There were ceramic trees with little brightly colored
lights, a silly elf hanging from mistletoe over the living room entry way,
decals on the windows, with an old, stately manger scene presiding over
it all. My sister, Becky, and I especially loved this ice skating rink with
tiny magnetic skaters you could move over the rink. I used to love to
play my mom's Christmas records on the big stereo in the living room.

We always baked lots of Christmas cookies. I particularly liked to make Thanksgiving and Christmas cookie cut-outs to bake and frost. I was very particular about these cut-outs. For Thanksgiving, it was white, tan, and orange turkeys. For Christmas, it was green trees, blue stars, white snowmen, and pink bells. They're a lot of work, but they sure are good. I have been searching for the perfect sugar cookie recipe for as long as I can remember.

We didn't spend a lot of money on Halloween. I was usually a ghost, courtesy of an old white sheet. My dream was always to wear a specific princess costume. This princess costume was sold in a box and came with a thin plastic mask that you attached to your face with a tiny rubber band that was stapled to the sides of the mask and was destined to break before the end of the night. One particularly memorable Halloween, when I was a little ghost as usual, I had a very embarrassing incident at school. It was exciting to bring your costume to school with the promise of donning it at the end of the day for a school-wide parade. We would go to the older kids' classrooms (where dressing up in school was beneath them), and parade through their rooms to the delight of teachers and students who would ooh and awe over the clever and cute little princesses and superheroes. I remember it well. The desks were arranged in groups of four around the big 6th grade room. I had my ghost sheet in place with round holes for two eyes and my nose. I was thoroughly enjoying the experience, floating around the room in single file with my classmates, when to my horror, my sheet became slightly askew, obscuring my vision. In my panic, I couldn't get the sheet adjusted with the three holes properly in place. I was bumping into desks, turning around and around. I didn't know which was the right way to go anymore was. I could hear kids laughing, and I could feel hands on me trying to right my costume and send me in the right direction again as I continued to bump off the desks and kids. It is funny to me now, but I was humiliated in the moment, saved only by the thought that no one could see my face anyway.

At Christmas my mom would hide our presents, and my sister Becky and I would search and search for them leading up to Christmas Day. My mom always tried hard to find just the right gifts to give everyone, and she was always saying, "I don't think I have enough yet." She would even count the presents to make sure it was fair.

We would wake up too early Christmas Day, and our parents would keep sending us back to bed. One Christmas morning I quietly made my way out to the living room to find the most beautiful lavender baby doll cradle under the tree. I was so excited to see it resting beneath the lit tree. I thought it was the most beautiful thing I had ever seen. It made a little tinkling sound when you rocked it. I also remember a gray stuffed poodle with a pink bow around its neck that I was so proud of. One year I got a white stuffed dog that had a radio in it. My mom would fill our stockings with toiletries and fun little gifts. We could each open one gift on Christmas Eve, and the best was when I would get a new, pretty nightgown to wear. We'd leave our opened gifts under the tree for the next week, making the fun last.

My mom made each of us a birthday cake, whatever kind we wanted. I always chose white cake and white or pink frosting. My mom always made sure we had the right number of candles on hand. Now I can't bear to think of buying my own girls' birthday cakes because I want the pleasure of making their cakes.

Here's another story about how my mom always made holidays special. One year when I lived in Elizabethtown, PA, my car broke down the night before I was to drive home to Binghamton, NY to celebrate Thanksgiving. I called my parents and told them I wasn't sure if my car would be ready the next day, or even how I was going to get to work in the morning. I went to bed that night praying for a solution and awoke to a knock on the apartment door early in the morning. There stood my parents with a bag of doughnuts. They took me to work, helped me pick up my car at the end of the day, and then we drove home to Binghamton for Thanksgiving. My mom even cleaned my apartment while I was at work, which at the time included cleaning out my rabbit cage. They didn't think anything of getting up in the middle of the night, driving 6 hours to take me to work and make sure I could get home for Thanksgiving. Holidays with family are special!

My mom hid our Easter baskets around the house, and to our constant surprise, she was a really good hider. We colored Easter eggs for our baskets, and my mom filled them up with lots of candy. We had a new dress to wear on every Easter Sunday. There's a picture of me wearing a frilly blue and white dress one Easter, standing outside our house with the daffodils in bloom.

My mom and I would watch figure skating together on TV. She would buy fun snacks for us to enjoy, and make an afternoon or evening special. She didn't save celebrating for just the big holidays. More than once my mom tried to get me to play hooky from school. Since she worked in the evening, she wanted me to take the day off to spend together. She would offer a day of shopping and eating out. Alas, I liked school too much to give in. Today, that seems ridiculous to me, but as a child I could not fathom skipping school.

We would go to the Ice Capades and circus at the arena whenever they were in town. I think my mom enjoyed the Ice Capades as much as we did. We would sometimes buy the big program, and of course, lots of snacks. I also remember surprise trips. My parents would not tell us where we were going. We would just head out on the road. One time we went to Howe Caverns, NY. It was lots of fun when we could bring a friend too.

Neither my husband nor I had a fireplace growing up, so when we started looking to buy a home, this was a special requirement for us. Then, it became a challenge to decorate the fireplace mantel. I tried different pictures and knick-knacks, but nothing was working. Then, one day it hit me that I could decorate the mantel for the seasons. I have always loved changing the living room around every few months, so getting to put up a new display on the mantel every few months is very exciting for our family. January and February get Valentine's Day decorations, March through May is Easter, June through August is patriotic, and September through November is fall and Thanksgiving, followed of course, by December in all its Christmas glory. I think of my mom and all her decorations each time I get out the boxes and make the big change. I look forward to the day when my girls are old enough to help with the decorating, because I just know they'll get a kick out of it. Of course, they try to help now, but it has involved a lot of super-glue after-the-fact on my part.

So, what do I choose to learn from my mom, that I want to pass on to my girls? First, she taught me to find your gift and use it. My mother's gift is taking care of sick and dying people. I hope that my girls are able to recognize what their gifts are. I think it is easier to see gifts in others, so I look forward to helping them find their gifts and be happy in a lifetime of expressing them. Now, I could have said compassion was the legacy I wanted to learn from my mom, because certainly it takes a great deal of compassion and humility to physically care for others, but I didn't want to miss the root of this gift: knowing what her talent was and using it. God gives us each gifts. I have no doubt that this job of my mom's was a gift God chose to give her. Jeremiah 1:4-5 boldly, proudly proclaims, "The word of the Lord came to me, saying, 'Before I formed you in the womb I knew you, before you were born I set you apart'" (NIV). Again, in Jeremiah 29:11, we see a God who has plans for His creation, "For I know the plans I have for you,' declares the Lord, 'plans to prosper you and not to harm you, plans to give you hope and a future'" (NIV). When I think of the daunting task of finding your mission in life, I am greatly reassured by Romans 8:31, "What shall we then say to these things? If God be for us, who can be against us?" (KJV).

Second, my mom taught me to celebrate the holidays, the seasons, birthdays, anything you can find to celebrate! This is a wonderful way to enjoy life, especially with your family. It is a way to mark the passing of time, and the perfect way to create memories. The Old Testament is full of festivals used to help God's people remember how He acted and provided for them. The call to celebration of Psalm 150 with its trumpets, dance, and clashing cymbals should leave little room for doubt that God appreciates the act of celebration. I remember when my mother baked a birthday cake for Jesus at Christmas, a tradition I now enjoy with my children. It was a good reminder that this is a Christian holiday with an important purpose. We need to remember and meditate on God's incredible goodness to us, every day, but especially at Christmas and Easter.

Legacy Commitment

1. I respect my mother for nursing sick and dying people.
- I admire her for finding something she is good at and using it to help many people throughout her life.
- I choose to learn from her, and begin to identify my gift and how I can use it to help people.
- I will closely watch my children, look for their gifts and talents, and encourage them to identify their gifts and use them to help others.

2. I love how my mother decorated the house for all the holidays, how she celebrated all the birthdays and holidays, but also the little things, like a special movie night. These are among my most vivid childhood memories.

- I choose to learn from my mom, and decorate and celebrate the big and little things in life all year long, every year.
- I will create memories of holidays, birthdays, and special events with my children.

Thinking About Our Legacies

The famous mystery writer, Agatha Christie, was born in 1890. In her autobiography, Christie reflected on the side effects of women's rights. She said,

> The position of women, over the years, has definitely changed for the worse. We women have behaved like mugs. We have clamoured to be allowed to work as men work. Men, not being fools, have taken kindly to the idea. Why support a wife? What's wrong with a wife supporting *herself*? She *wants* to do it. By Golly, she can go on doing it! It seems sad that having established ourselves so cleverly as the 'weaker sex,' we should now be broadly on par with the women of primitive tribes who toil in the fields all day. (Christie, 1977, p. 131)[1]

As soon as I read that, coming from a successful and intelligent woman with book sales literally in the billions, I felt she was on to something. Women work full time while raising children and taking care of a house, trying to balance out conflicting responsibilities, dealing with stress, and heartache. I don't think it is too far reaching to say my heart aches every morning when I leave for work and my little ones' faces are looking up at me. If they are happy and playing, I am sad because they are so content without me, and if they are sad and crying, I am heart-broken to have to leave them. Of course, I know they are fine after I leave, but I am not fine. I don't want it all. I think some women might, but I don't honestly know. Now, I have a PhD, so it is not that I am looking for an easy way

---

1 From *Agatha Christie: An Autobiography*, by A. Christie, 1977, New York, NY: HarperCollins.

out of the workforce. I believe God created women to take care of their children. I feel I didn't have children to give them to someone else to raise. My husband and I have been able to work opposite schedules so that we have not used a day care so far, but that is kind of like being a single parent, which is not easy either. My mother always had to work with four children to raise, and I can now begin to appreciate what that is like. So, there will be no complaints about my childhood, no bad words about my mother, no negative thoughts. I believe I had a relatively good childhood, but I also believe we can choose what to reflect on, what to learn from our mothers, and what to pass on to our children. Parenting is not an easy job, and this is not a perfect world.

It might not be popular to say, but since I am going out on a limb anyway to ponder and proclaim the legacies I want to leave my children, one of my hopes for my girls is that they will be blessed with children that they can stay home with and raise, without having to leave for work and hire babysitters every day. With this is mind, I need to spend less time and money at Target on things we don't need, and save up for their college and any way I can help prepare them for independent lives. No one talked about the burden of starting adult life with student loan debt when I was younger, or perhaps I just wasn't listening. I plan to actively teach them how to live within their means, to use a budget, to set goals, and plan ahead. The scary part is that I will need to model this for them. I recognize that each of my girls are individuals who will have their own thoughts and ideas, and I know that many mothers successfully and seemingly happily work outside of the home, so I do not know if this is something that will be important to them, but I still can't help thinking about it.

In December, 2013, I left my job of 14 years to stay home with my girls. I cried many times during the final weeks of that job, leaving behind fond memories and fun coworkers and friends. It was an answer to prayer that God brought me to the point where I could work from home teaching online, and not need to leave my girls every day. When I was working outside my home, I did not have the energy and discipline to raise my children with these legacies in mind. I was just getting through each day. During the first week home, I had the thought, how do people work full time and get all this done? Now, there is no excuse. Each day I need to work toward my goal of leaving spiritual legacies.

I know there are women with sad childhoods with no good memories, and no positive legacies to glean from their mothers. It is possible to learn from a bad role model how we want to ensure we do not behave as mothers, but that forces us to think negatively which can be depressing. Perhaps, there has been someone in your life who was like a mother to you? Isaiah 49:15-16 asks,

> Never! Can a mother forget her nursing child? Can she feel no love for the child she has borne? But even if that were possible, I would not forget you! See, I have written your name on the palms of my hands. (NLT)

If that doesn't convince you that God can be your mother, look at Zephaniah 3:17, "The Lord your God is with you, he is mighty to save. He will take great delight in you, he will quiet you with his love, he will rejoice over you with singing" (NLT). I have two favorite memories in my head that I occasionally bring to mind, and they makes me smile every time. The first is the moment when the nurse in my delivery room placed my baby girls in my arms just after they were born. It makes me cry just thinking about it. The second is how my baby girls would mold themselves around the front of me when they fell asleep on the Boppy pillow on my lap. It was such a great feeling, and I would think about how much I loved them every single time. When I think of how much I love my children, and I know that God in His perfect love, loves me more, I am completely blown away. I love the image of God quieting me with His love and rejoicing over me with singing, because I can relate so perfectly to this image, having enjoyed this same scene over and over with my children.

If you have no happy memories or legacies from your mom, God will be your perfect Mom. I don't think it's wrong to picture Him this way. After all, He shared this tender image of a mom nursing her child, and he created us in His image. What mom and dad hasn't sat around gazing at their child and thought, "We created that? Amazing." Psalm 139:13 reminds us, "you knit me together in my mother's womb" (NIV). There are two things I believed before I had children, but they were really brought home to me after my girls were born. First, my babies were alive inside me from the moment of conception. Second, God created us. This is not chance. This is amazing design.

Take some time to think about your mother and what legacies she has passed on to you. What do you admire about your mother? If you were limited to two positive sentences to share with your children about your own mother, what would you write? Can you see how these items have shaped who you are today? Don't worry if you can't, because identifying what you want to say about your mother, what you want to focus on passing on to your children, can help you now actively choose to shape your life in this way.

Legacy Scripture Verses to Commit to Memory

"'For I know the plans I have for you,' declares the Lord, 'plans to prosper you and not to harm you, plans to give you hope and a future'" (Jeremiah 29:11 NIV).

Likewise the Spirit helps us in our weakness. For we do not know what to pray for as we ought, but the Spirit himself intercedes for us with groaning too deep for words. And he who searches hearts knows what is the mind of the Spirit, because the Spirit intercedes for the saints according to the will of God. And we know that for those who love God all things work together for good, for those who are called according to his purpose. For those whom he foreknew he also predestined to be conformed to the image of his Son, in order that he might be the firstborn among many brothers. And those whom he predestined he also called, and those whom he called he also justified, and those whom he justified he also glorified. What then shall we say to these things? If God is for us, who can be against us? (Romans 8:26-31 ESV)

"For you created my inmost being; you knit me together in my mother's womb" (Psalm 139:13 NIV).

See Also
Jeremiah 1:4-5
Psalm 150
Isaiah 49:15-16
Zephaniah 3:17

Chapter 2

My Dad: Faith and Reading

I honestly did not have to think long to come up with the legacies I have gained from my father. When I pray before meals, trips, and bed, I think of my dad. When I look around the house and see the bookshelves he made me stocked and overflowing with books, many that he bought me, I think of my dad. I recommend that you note the first things that come to mind when you think of your dad. Think of the best things about the person you are remembering. What are your favorite qualities that you see in that person?

Faith

I do not think I am alone in thinking that faith is what defines my dad. It is not something he does on Sunday, but who he is every day of the week. I want to be transparent with my children about my faith, beliefs, and spirituality.

One of my favorite people in the Bible is Daniel. It is easy to be judgmental when a person's sins are laid out for everyone to read about, and the Bible is full of sinners. I have always admired Daniel because there are no lies, jealous thoughts, or other sins recorded here, though of course we know "for all have sinned and fall short of the glory of God" (Romans 3:23 NIV). I wonder what Daniel's parents were like? How outrageous is this: in Daniel 6:4-5 it states that when the jealous political leaders were looking for something wrong in Daniel's life to accuse him of, the only thing they could find was how he worshipped his God. Can you imagine if someone said that about you? I've struggled with a big mouth, and unkind thoughts and words for as long as I can remember, and I'm sure if someone was trying really hard to find something bad to say about me, it could be done. (Alright, even without trying hard.)

I don't see how Daniel could have just naturally been that faithful. I wonder if there were godly parents in his background who helped to set him up for success for the rest of his life. By which I mean a spotless reputation and an unwavering faith in God and His promises. Now, that's a legacy. I want to be a part of shaping my children's personalities, protecting their reputations, and teaching and nurturing their faith in God. I want to be a mom of a Daniel (or Danielle, in my situation).

Lois is an older person's name. It's just a fact. My whole life when I tell someone my name, I invariably hear, "oh, that's my grandmother's name." My husband likes to tell the story of how his friends asked him how old I was when they heard my name was Lois. Check out 2 Timothy 1:5 where even then it was a grandmother's name, "I am reminded of your sincere faith, a faith that dwelt first in your grandmother Lois and your mother Eunice and now, I am sure, dwells in you as well" (ESV). I'm going to take my namesake's example and be a woman of faith, and raise children of faith, like Daniel.

I grew up learning the Bible, and accepted Jesus as my Savior when I was still very young. I simply always believed the Bible is God's Word. I believe His promises, so why haven't I been able to claim all of His promises? I pondered this concept of faith, until I remembered the song, Trust and Obey, by John Sammis, that I used to love singing as a little girl. It really says it all. For me, the knowledge and belief part of faith is easier than the trusting and obeying.

Trust And Obey

When we walk with the Lord in the light of His Word,
What a glory He sheds on our way!
While we do His good will, He abides with us still,
And with all who will trust and obey.

Not a shadow can rise, not a cloud in the skies,
But His smile quickly drives it away;
Not a doubt or a fear, not a sigh or a tear,
Can abide while we trust and obey.

Not a burden we bear, not a sorrow we share,
But our toil He doth richly repay;
Not a grief or a loss, not a frown or a cross,
But is blessed if we trust and obey.

But we never can prove the delights of His love
Until all on the altar we lay;
For the favor He shows, for the joy He bestows,
Are for them who will trust and obey.

Then in fellowship sweet we will sit at His feet.
Or we'll walk by His side in the way.
What He says we will do, where He sends we will go;
Never fear, only trust and obey.

Trust and obey, for there's no other way
To be happy in Jesus, but to trust and obey.

When I think of faith, three different ideas come to mind: believe, obey, and trust. First is my faith in God the Father, God the Son, and God the Holy Spirit. Having been blessed to be brought up in a Christian home, I do not remember ever not having this kind of faith. People from all different backgrounds seem to be at least somewhat familiar with John 3:16: "For God so loved the world, that He gave His only begotten Son, that whosoever believeth in Him should not perish, but have everlasting life" (KJV). Perhaps people are too familiar with this verse, and miss the profound message of faith it contains.

I pray for my children to come to know Jesus with child-like faith, for I truly think it is easier to believe in a divine Creator and Savior, than evolution and no certainty of life after death. My girls are both very young now, but I plan to mark the dates they pray and accept God's gift of salvation. How great will it be for them to be able to remember and celebrate those dates?

Of course faith is more than just believing and making a personal profession of faith. When I was a little girl I mistakenly thought I had to pray and ask God to save me and to come into my heart every time I sinned. I distinctly recall sitting in the backyard at home praying, begging God to save me yet again, when I suddenly knew I was saved forever, meaning I was God's child for all eternity. God seemed to be speaking to me, telling me forgiveness is what I was meant to be praying for, and that my fear of being condemned to hell was wrong. This must have been my first revelation that God, the Holy Spirit, indeed lives in us, that faith is a living, breathing, amazing part of who I am. So, the second part of faith for me, is the action, the "obey" of trust and obey. While the believing part of faith seems to come easy for me, the obeying part is considerably more involved. Joshua 1:7-9 contains the secret to success: obedience to and meditation on God's Word. Have you ever heard someone say, "if only God would speak to me, and tell me His will for my life," or "Just tell me exactly what to do God." Of course, He did that in the Old Testament, and it is pretty clear how that worked out for people. The thing is, we have His Word in the form of the Bible. Faith means reading, meditating, and obeying the Bible. You have to know what the Bible teaches in order to obey God.

Growing up, we went to church every time the doors were open. There was Sunday School and Junior Church on Sunday morning, and then the Sunday evening service. There was prayer meeting on Wednesday evening, and Bible club, called AWANA, on Monday night. Nowadays, many people could never imagine going to church that much. It is ironic that with all the time-saving devices available to us now, we are busier than ever. Church is family for Christians, and an obvious means for us to learn God's Word, which teaches "not forsaking the assembling of ourselves together, as the manner of some is; but exhorting one another: and so much the more, as ye see the day approaching" (Hebrews 10:25 KJV), and "for where two or three are gathered together in my name, there am I in the midst of them" (Matthew 18:20 KJV). I am thankful for the priority my parents placed on attending church.

In the same way that we do not attend as much church as we used to, I don't think people memorize the Bible the way believers did in the past. I think we have deceived ourselves that we are incapable of memorizing a lot of verses, chapters, or even books of the Bible, or at least that we don't have the time to. Maybe it's a lost art. For example, no one even memorizes phone numbers anymore. You just put the number in your phone, and you never have to recall those seven digits again. As an adult, I appreciate the many Bible verses I learned in AWANA, including the books of the Bible. We struggle in so many areas of our lives, when we have this amazing resource in the Bible, if we would only commit ourselves to the tasks of memorization and meditation.

That we can talk to God anytime, anywhere is mind-boggling. First Thessalonians 5:17 tells us to "pray without ceasing" (ESV). If we are living faithfully, obeying God's Word to us, then we are reading the Bible, memorizing verses to meditate on, going to church, and praying; surely if we live these acts of faith we will be sensitive to the will of God in our lives. I have read a number of helpful books on prayer, and my conclusion is that the best way to begin is to just start talking to God; do not set out to make it over complicated. At first, it feels awkward and unpracticed, especially praying in front of others, but knowing that God will help us, teach us, and bring us along in the faith, is encouraging, not to mention that experiencing His answers to prayer is certainly uplifting. It was unnerving when my 3 year old accused me of copying her Sunday School teacher when I prayed with her or she saw me reading the Bible. I don't want my children to see anything unordinary about me praying or reading the Bible. I have to get into the practice of talking openly with my children, and others, about my faith.

In addition to believing and obeying, for me the most challenging aspect of faith is trusting. The great news is that the Bible has a lot of encouraging words on trusting God. What is clear from Scripture is that trust begins in the mind. Isaiah 26:3 promises, "Thou wilt keep him in perfect peace whose mind is stayed on Thee: because he trusteth in Thee" (KJV). We are reassured that God will direct our paths when we trust Him and not ourselves (Proverbs 3:5-6).

It is as simple as Psalm 23:1, "The Lord is my Shepherd, I shall not want" (ESV). The promises of providing and answering our prayers are there if we have the faith: Psalm 34:9-10, Psalm 37:3-5, Mark 11:22-24, Mark 9:23.

Reading

My dad's books fill shelves and every spare space in my parents' house. If my dad is sitting down, he has a book in his hands. Every vacation meant extra time for him to read. When he visits us now, I like to find a new book for him each time. What a great legacy to pass on!

I enjoyed reading the classics. Growing up, there was a used paperback book store near us where I could exchange books. I loved Charles Dickens from the first sentence of *David Copperfield, Great Expectations, Bleak House*, and of course, *A Christmas Carol*. That led me to George Eliot's *Daniel Deronda, Silas Marner,* and *Middlemarch*. I liked being transported to a different time and place with diverse characters with fun names, tragedies, and triumphs. I went through a period of Russian novels by Dostoyevsky and Tolstoy which depressed me after a while. I read *War and Peace* and *Les Miserables*, and hated to even get up to use the bathroom between pages. My eyes would hurt from being so tired and from crying, but I couldn't put those books down. Sometimes, I would purposely read a book slowly, savoring the story, trying to make it last as long as possible. This was necessary with all of Jane Austen's novels. I am still not sure if all those dreamy, other world books did me any good, or harm in the long run. My husband and I are both big readers, and we hope that our girls will be too.

I thought it would be fun and easy to come up with a list of books I want to be sure to have my girls read, but I found this to be a much more difficult task than I imagined. This is mostly because the classics and novels I read when I was younger are not fresh in my mind anymore. Now I start to wonder just how helpful and meaningful were all those books I read growing up? You don't think so much about the message of books you read as a child, or how they might be shaping and influencing your life, at least I don't remember doing so. We always had books all over the house. I still have a set of the *Little House on the Prairie* books that were my sister Becky's and then mine as a girl. I used to love going to the church library and signing out lots of books each week. My dad and I both liked the Christian prairie romance novels, and I kept my favorite Janette Oaks books for my children to enjoy some day. I loved the *Chronicles of Narnia* by C. S. Lewis. I want to be sure to pass on the biographies of George Muller, Amy Carmichael, and Corrie Ten Boom to my girls.

My dad's legacies are faith and reading. Put God first in your life. Go to church, spend time with other Christians, read the Bible, memorize and meditate on Scripture, pray. My dad always hated to miss church, no matter how tired or ill he might be. When I picture my Dad, I see him sitting at the kitchen table reading the Bible early in the morning. I do not pretend to write an encompassing chapter on faith here, but it has been a good practice to stop and really think about what the definition of faith is, what it means to me, so that I can plan to pass this on to my children.

Legacy Commitment

1. I respect my father as a man of faith who reads his Bible every morning, goes to church every week, and prays before every meal and trip.
- I choose to be a woman of faith, like my namesake, and set a great example for my children.
- I will raise children of faith, like Daniel.
2. I love how my dad is always reading a book.
- I will take time to read as often as possible.
- I will share with my children the best books, starting with the Bible.

Thinking About Our Legacies

I can't imagine a life without reading, and I hope my girls will both love to read, because books bring the world, past and present, to you. If you had to list ten books you want your children to read that made an impression on you, or that you wish you had read as a child, what would those books be? What does faith mean to you, and how will you go about passing your faith on to your children?

If your earthly father did not leave you a spiritual legacy, we are comforted by our heavenly Father who calls us His children (Romans 8:15, 2 Corinthians 6:18). First John 3:1 has always been a favorite verse of mine: "Behold, what manner of love the Father hath bestowed upon us, that we should be called the sons of God: therefore the world knoweth us not, because it knew Him not" (KJV). I am amazed by God's love for me, and amazed that He calls me His child. The third part of this verse reminds me I am supposed to be different as a child of God, different from the world.

How can we continue to honor our parents as adults? Certainly, we need to watch how we talk in front of our children about our parents/ their grandparents. We are modeling for our children how to respect and honor parents. If this is difficult, think about how we will want our children to treat us when they are adults.

I have yet to find the person who feels he or she has too much time on their hands. As our parents retire, and things get even busier for us as parents of young children, we need to work harder to include parents in our lives with cards, phone calls, and visits. As we think about the legacies our parents have left us that we want to continue to shape our lives and our children's lives, we can be purposeful about how we talk about our parents to our children, emphasizing these positive legacies.

Legacy Scripture Verses to Commit to Memory

"Trust in the Lord with all your heart and lean not on your own understanding; in all your ways acknowledge him, and He will make your paths straight" (Proverbs 3:5-6 NIV).

"Trust in the Lord and do good; dwell in the land and enjoy safe pasture. Delight yourself in the Lord and He will give you the desires of your heart" (Psalm 37:3-4 NIV).

See Also
Daniel 6:4-5
2 Timothy 1:5
Joshua 1:7-9
1 Thessalonians 5:17
Isaiah 26:3
Psalm 23:1
Psalm 34:9-10
Mark 11:22-24
Mark 9:23
Romans 8:15
2 Corinthians 6:18
1 John 3:1

Chapter 3

My Grandma Wagner: Home and Rejoice

I have wonderful memories of my Grandma Wagner, and I am very thankful that my parents made regular trips to her house when we were growing up. Her house and garden are etched in my mind with an almost magical quality. I see my children adoring their grandparents in a similar way now. I think it is perfectly fine to share your perhaps idealized memories of loved ones, because youth is a time when if we are blessed, we see the beauty and magic around us, not the dust, shortcomings, or inconveniences.

What did we all do before home and garden television shows that guide the average family? Well to start, we had a two-toned light blue and royal blue shag rug in our living room growing up. Other than bedrooms, most rooms had white walls. My sister, Holly, had a mint green bedroom. I don't remember my mom going through any particular collecting phase or anything that could be defined as a decorating style. My mom has always liked garage sales, and I have always not liked garage sales. Over the years, things came in, and little went out. My husband likes what he calls a "homey, lived-in feel," but I dislike what I consider "cluttered and overwhelming." I remember it was common to have doilies on the back and arms of chairs, and plastic runners spread across the living room floor to protect that special blue shag rug. I distinctly recall cords running across ceilings and walls at my grandmother's house.

We often went to my grandmas' houses. Grandma Wagner lived in Silver Creek, NY. I loved going to her house by the creek. Even the name, Silver Creek, sounded special. Grandma Wagner had closets full of clothes and shoes, and boxes of fun jewelry. She kept a cart next to the kitchen table that held all kinds of make-up, a gold mine for us as children. We would dress up and play all over the house. There were three bedrooms upstairs. My parents stayed in the large bedroom with windows overlooking the main street in town. The granddaughters would take turns staying in what we called the "little room." It was a very pretty bedroom with a single bed and a dressing table with boxes of jewelry underneath, another amazing gold mine. It was our favorite room. The other room two girls shared had a double bed with a beautiful lavender bedspread. There was a locked cabinet in there where we imagined all kinds of treasures hid. As much as we loved to have the little bedroom, it was still fun to share the purple bedroom.

There are some pictures from our dress-up adventures. My sister Becky is wearing a yellow dress in one, holding a rose. One time my sister Holly did my makeup, and it would not come off with anything. I had mascara all over my face for a week.

We would play card games on the floor of the parlor, a fancy room we rarely went in. My Grandma Wagner had a huge salt and pepper shaker collection she kept in the cabinets in the parlor. There was a back room behind the kitchen that was full of clothes. She had a big bathtub, but no shower, which seemed so strange to us. Grandma Wagner had a pantry which I thought was really neat because I don't think I had ever seen one anywhere else before. She would disappear in there and come out with all sorts of special treats for us.

What do you remember eating at your grandmother' house? We loved the toast at Grandma Wagner's house. Now, we imagine it's because my Grandma used real butter and we weren't used to such a luxury, but at the time we had no idea why the toast was so good there. (I think my parents must have been buying margarine at the time.) Grandma Wagner had goober grape jelly with the peanut butter mixed in one jar, and that was pretty special too. I can still see my Grandma coming out of that pantry with a plate of buttered toast for us.

Grandma Wagner had beautiful roses all around her house. The spectacular gardens added to the magical feeling of being there. The plastic pink flamingos and swans seemed to fit in just fine there. We would wade up and down the creek beside her house and play in the little water falls all day. It was a beautiful home and yard.

Grandma Wagner would take us shopping to pick out little gifts for us. One year for Christmas she bought me a Barbie doll, and what must surely have been absolutely every outfit accessory that you could buy for a Barbie doll. Her house was covered in pictures of all of her family. I don't remember at what age I first heard that my Grandma Wagner had adopted my mom, her niece.

I remember Grandma Wagner as a very special lady. She was a talented gardener. I always felt very loved by her. She was so happy to see us, and so sad to see us go. I think it is very special that she made her house such a fantastic, fun, wonderful place to be, that I still remember it vividly with great fondness so many years later.

She wore make-up, dyed hair, and wore heals and jewelry every day of her life. I want to dress for every day like it's special, love and treat everyone like they're special, and grow lots of flowers just like my Grandma Wagner.

Home

I think a garden is a wonderful way to experience God's beautiful creation. It is hard work, but the smells and sights are incomparable. What a wonderful way to surround yourself with beautiful things. Grandma Wagner took special care of her garden, her home, and her appearance. I like how she dressed up for every day. Take some pride in your appearance, but not too much! I think it's a nice way to make a day special, by dressing up for it, taking the time to put some jewelry and make-up on. Again, it takes work, but I think it's a good reminder that every day is special. I don't know how Grandma Wagner created such a special home that has stayed so vividly in my mind. I can still smell the baby powder she used in the bathroom, the roses in the yard, and the stuffed peppers cooking in the kitchen.

Rejoice

Philippians 4:4-9 which begins, "Rejoice in the Lord always. I will say it again: Rejoice!" (NIV), is the perfect perspective on life. When I think about how to bring joy into the lives of my children, one thing I am sure of is that it is not about stuff. So, why don't I always realize this for myself? My three year old has a lovely way of reviewing her day. She'll say something like "I had a good time playing at the playground with you and Julia. That was fun. Remember when that boy sat on the train with us?" I feel I can learn from her and this simple task of reviewing the daily pleasures. She makes me feel great when she repeatedly talks about what a good time she had. A trip to the grocery store is special to her. I have learned from my kids how to enjoy special moments together, review them with each other, and savor the joy a little longer.

My husband and I were recently talking about how kids adore animals. Taking in God's creation is a wonderful way to experience joy. My grandmother's beautiful garden brought her , and anyone who passed by, joy. I wonder if God enjoys hearing our words of amazement and praise for His creation. I suppose most people do not spend a great deal of time praising God for their own physical bodies, but it is easy to do when you watch your children develop and grow before your eyes. There is constant amazement and joy in the incredible journey from the womb on.

Enjoy the special moments in life; review these moments together with your loved ones; enjoy God's creation —His animals, plants, and people; and last, but certainly not least, count your blessings. I have to admit, I honestly miss singing some of the hymns I grew up with. I cannot think of rejoicing over God's blessings without hymns like, "There Shall be Showers of Blessings," and "Count Your Blessings." There may be no greater way to rejoice in the Lord always, than to start listing off your blessings. I am completely flabbergasted by God's blessings in my life. There should be nothing but joy when I consider God's mercy and grace toward me.

As I ponder the legacies of those in my life, I am intrigued by how big a part the mind and choice play in our lives. The choice to rejoice starts with what we think about, what we choose to dwell on, what we fill our minds with, and then what pours out of our mouths. The music we listen to, the television we watch, the books we read, the people we spend time with will all affect our level of rejoicing. I used to think inspirational books and speakers were silly because it seemed to me so temporary. I thought that people would get motivated in the moment, and then fall back into old ways. Somewhere I read a response to this criticism that pointed out one needs to take a shower every day because you will get dirty again. We need to keep going back for inspiration, back to the music and books that keep us rejoicing.

As Christians, we can rejoice in the past, present, and future. James 4:14 reminds us of the brevity of life. We need to have joy in the moment, and not live constantly thinking about the future and the joy we could experience when or if only.

The Bible teaches us to practice hospitality (1 Peter 4:9 and Hebrews 13:2). I don't feel keeping a well-run home receives the respect it deserves in today's culture. It has become almost an insult to train girls in the art and science of housekeeping. There is so much emphasis put on higher education, starting a career, earning a prestigious job title, making a certain salary, and living a certain lifestyle. Perhaps we have forgotten that a well-run home takes skill and training. Cleaning, organizing, budgeting, maintaining a home, cooking, raising children…these are just a few of the countless chores found in homemaking.

We should not be ashamed of purposefully teaching our boys and girls how to keep well-run homes that we can use for God's glory. Of course we can go too far and spend too much time, money, and concern caring for our houses and yards. Time spent cleaning and gardening can be therapeutic, and can be a wonderful occasion for spending time in prayer. At the same time, we cannot let a spotless house or immaculate yard become a god, and take the place of other meaningful tasks in our lives.

I remember one pediatrician visit when I was embarrassed about my two year old's bruises and dirty feet. My wise doctor said he wanted to see kids with little scrapes and some dirt because healthy kids should be outside playing and having fun. I recall this whenever I clean, brush, lotion, and dress my little angels only to see all that hard work undone so quickly by a snack or romp in the backyard.

Often when I wash all the beautiful windows in our living room and dining area, at least one of my kids follows behind, either "helping" me clean or just resting a pudgy little hand on the window, watching my progress. I have to continually remind myself what is important. Learning balance is critical to keeping house and raising children. After all, I think most people suspect when an outfit or hairdo was probably not the mom's doing. Sometimes, you just have to go with the flow, because it is far more important what your children and God think about how you handle these little challenges, than what friends, family, or strangers think of you.

Legacy Commitment

1. My Grandma Wagner's house after all these years still seems like a magical place to me.
- I will make my home and yard special, the kind of place people enjoy visiting.
- I will teach my children to keep a clean, organized, well-decorated home. We will spend time in the garden together, learning to tend the flowers.
2. I have fond memories of my Grandma Wagner and her house.
- I like how she dressed up for life every day. I will make an effort to make every day special. I will not save clothes or jewelry for a special occasion.
- I will teach my children the importance and benefit of dressing up for life and making every day special.

Thinking About Our Legacies

Do you have a grandmother you remember fondly? My own memories of Grandmother Wagner are a good reminder to me to make every effort to provide my children with lots of opportunities to make lasting, loving memories with their grandparents. I like nice jewelry, but how often do I take the time to select something to wear? What can you do to make every day special? What can you do to make your home and yard the kind of place people enjoy visiting?

"This is the day the Lord hath made: we will rejoice and be glad in it" (Psalm 118:24 KJV), deserves to be framed and strategically placed where I will see it every morning. As you start to uncover your spiritual legacies some will stick out to you as particularly significant. Are there one or two verses you might want to print and frame as constant reminders? Of course you can always do an online search and buy the verse already framed, but I could not find exactly what I was looking for. As it turns out, I think the extra effort of finding nice paper and a frame and making my own picture was good for me.

Legacy Scripture Verses to Commit to Memory

"Offer hospitality to one another without grumbling" (I Peter 4:9 NIV).

"Do not forget to entertain strangers, for by so doing some people have entertained angels without knowing it" (Hebrews 13:2 NIV).

"This is the day which the Lord hath made; we will rejoice and be glad in it" (Psalm 118:24 KJV).

Rejoice in the Lord always. I will say it again: Rejoice! Let your gentleness be evident to all. The Lord is near. Do not be anxious about anything, but in everything, by prayer and petition with thanksgiving, present your request to God. And the peace of God, which transcends all understanding, will guard your hearts and your minds in Christ Jesus. Finally, brothers, whatever is trued, whatever is noble, whatever is right, whatever is pure, whatever is lovely, whatever is admirable—if anything is excellent or praiseworthy—think about such things. Whatever you have learned or received from me, or seen in me—put into practice. And the God of peace will be with you. (Philippians 4:4-9 NIV)

Chapter 4

My Grandma Campbell: Simplicity and Love

I loved both sets of my grandparents, but I appreciate the differences that I noticed when I wrote about them here. That is a benefit of writing about multiple people who have been a part of your life. Can you embrace simplicity and have trays of make-up and boxes of jewelry? I don't know, but I'm going to try. I hope that you have someone in your journal who personifies love, because it is our greatest achievement.

We visited Grandma Campbell in Penn Yan, NY where she lived in a trailer that we would all stuff into together. There was a five-and-dime store by her house that we could walk to and buy lots of fun candy from. My brother spent every cent he could find there.

My Grandma Campbell lived simply and quietly. There is something very sweet about seeing the love of a mama for her children, and I never had any doubt Grandma loved my dad. She was sweet and tough at the same time. She battled cancer, and yet I never heard her complain about anything or anyone. Sometimes, she would take the bus to visit us.

Simplicity

I am trying to figure out how to reconcile the legacies of home and simplicity. I hadn't really thought about it before, but my grandmothers were quite different from each other. I admire the jewelry wearing, high heeled, hair-dyed grandmother who kept a neat parlor in the front of her house, and I admire my grandma who lived in a small trailer and did not have boxes of jewelry and rooms full of clothes. I am glad to be contemplating a legacy of simplicity so soon after thinking about keeping a nice home.

My husband and I had cable for a couple of years, and I enjoyed the home and garden shows. When we cancelled the cable to save money, one benefit I felt was not being able to watch these home improvement shows which led to my feeling dissatisfied with my house. I don't feel there is anything wrong with these shows, except that for me I would look around and see all the changes I would make if I had the money. I would daydream about a finished basement, professional landscaping, and tiled backsplash in the kitchen, and that's just to name a few projects that went through my mind.

In reality, my husband, girls, and I are blessed with a beautiful home that more than meets our needs. The average size of a house in America has increased steadily through the years. According to the National Association of Home Builders, in 1970 the average household was 3.1 people living in a 1,500 square foot home. In 2007, 2.7 people lived in 2,400 square feet. In 2009 it was 2,700 square feet. So basically, if this was 1950 I would have a big house. How big a house do you need? How many bathrooms would make you happy? When did it become essential for mom and dad to have their own master bathroom? Why do we need closets we can walk into when most of us wear the same clothes all the time anyway? (And men need caves? Don't get me started on that one.)

I saw one home-buying show where a young couple bought a huge house with a gourmet kitchen that was a necessity. At the end of the show they showed the couple serving their guests a package of cookies and a bag of chips. Good thing they had granite countertops to whip those fancy hors' oeuvres up on.

I would like to propose a home improvement show where they go in and remove a bunch of stuff, and don't bring anything new in, don't renovate, just see how people like living with less stuff.

I refuse to take sole responsibility for all the stuff in our house. Loved ones are constantly giving us stuff, and a lot of that stuff is big. When I do find the time to clean out rooms and make a donation, it feels great to gain some space. So much stuff can get overwhelming.

It is a wonderful blessing to live in a prosperous country, and to have generous family and friends. Somehow we need to figure out how to keep things simple. How many toys do two little kids need? What is the point at which they can no longer appreciate what they have?

Have you ever experienced coming upon something you didn't realize you had, and thinking that would have come in handy last week? If you have so much stuff that you don't know what stuff you have, surely it must be too much stuff.

Living simply is in part about donating to others some of the surplus in our lives, but an even bigger challenge might be staying out of the stores to begin with. Bath and Body Works, Yankee Candle, and Target just call my name. Even a trip to the grocery store can get out of hand. So many people attest to the power of paying with cash to curb spending. This is one of my goals, but at the time of this writing, I admit I still am not there.

It is very important to me to pass a legacy of simplicity down to my girls. Obviously, the best way for me to do so is to model living simply myself. I could be in denial, but I think it is actually easier for me to live simply, than it is for me to help my girls live simply. When I look into their beautiful faces, and my heart just wells up with love, I want to buy them all kinds of things I think they might like. I have witnessed firsthand countless times how quickly they tire of some toy or snack they liked the week before.

Less is more has been a motto of mine for years, but simplicity means more to me than counting our toys. It is about enjoying simple pleasures in the moment, and later when we reflect. Like how my Grandma Campbell enjoyed her white powdered boxed donuts. She didn't need a delicate pastry from a fancy bakery. I'll admit I actually like boxed cake and canned frosting. There, I said it. (I can appreciate homemade cake too, for the record.) Sometimes, when things are less expensive we think we must be missing out, unless you are one of those rare breeds committed to frugality.

If saving money doesn't speak to you, maybe the ideas of recycling and not being wasteful are more appealing. I admit to being plain lazy at times when it comes to recycling and being mindful of how I use items. I want to raise children who do not waste water, food, and materials. I have so much room to grow in this area! No doubt we have all experienced how products do not last like they used to. It might be easier and more appealing to just throw something out and replace with brand new, but if it can be recycled, donated, or held onto, it is worth my efforts.

Simplicity is about contentment, satisfaction, and appreciation. Again, our mind and choices play such a big part in our lives. Matthew 6:21 puts it clearly, "For where your treasure is, there will your heart be also" (NIV). If I am listing off home improvement projects, looking at what others have, and day dreaming about what I want, I am wasting my life. I have to choose to list more worthy goals, for example, 1 Timothy 6:10-11.

The concepts of simplicity and love go together nicely. In 1 John 2:15-17 we are reminded not to love the world or the things in the world.

Love

Love…it certainly seems like a huge topic, but it is covered succinctly and convincingly in Matthew 22:37-39. Love God with all your heart, soul, and mind, then love your neighbor as yourself. When I think of my Grandma Campbell, I think of her love for my dad, which you could see written on her face at all times. She loved all of us, but she seemed to have a special fondness for my brother too, which was sweet.

In John 15:9-17, Jesus teaches us that if we keep His commandments, we abide in His love. If we are going to keep His commandments, then we need to be reading His Word to us in order to know how He wants us to live. If we love God, we will spend time talking to Him. Reading and meditating on the Bible, and praying seem like pretty obvious manifestations of our love for God, but of course, we need help from the Holy Spirit to understand God's Word and to know how to pray.

The Bible insists we cannot serve God and money. We cannot have two masters. Our love for God needs to be the number one priority in our lives. Who hasn't remarked, "I love chocolate," or "I love the Yankees?" Ok, maybe not those exact two statements, but I do think we throw around the word love. We can enjoy hobbies, sports, and food, but we are commanded to love God and people, and quite frankly, that's it. I'm going to check my use of the word love, and make sure my heart is in the right place, on the right Master and on what is important to Him—people.

More than anything I have heard people passionately and at great length and descriptiveness, discuss their love of…food! Have you ever been guilty of dreaming about vanilla bean cupcakes with mounds of buttercream frosting on top, or is that just me? I wonder how my life would change if I exchanged each thought about food with a thought of

God? After all, the Bible doesn't say draw near to food. We're to draw near to God. Whatever masters, even innocent pastimes that compete for my attention need to be put into perspective.

The greatest way we show God our love is in our love for each other. Jesus said in Mark 12:31, "Love your neighbor as yourself" (NIV). Now I know the popular current teaching is that people are at great risk for low self-esteem, and the mantra is to love yourself first. But you can't escape the fact that the Bible assumes we love ourselves. I do not pretend to be an expert on self-esteem. I will hazard to mention the possibility that some pride and envy masquerades as low self-esteem. Is it because we believe we deserve better that we feel so low about ourselves? Again, I am no expert, and I readily admit I have not experienced the abuses that can cause some people to feel self-misery. My value is in my identity as God's child (1 John 3:1).

I love God. I love His Word. I love my beautiful family. Now my pen slows down as I try to honestly name more people. Thank you Jesus for sending Your Holy Spirit, because I need help loving everyone. James wisely reminds us to love in action; it's not enough to declare our love in words. If I focus on my love for people, and spend less time dwelling on the little things I do not appreciate, I can begin to grow my love for others, with God's help. It is hard to pray for someone without coming to feel love for that person.

I am concerned that it might be a little-known fact that there is no place for prejudice in Christianity. We are not commanded to only love people who are most like us, or those closest to us, but to "love one another" (John 13:34-35 NIV), and even our enemies (Matthew 5:43-48). In another scenario, some of us struggle with love in action more toward those we are closest to than those we are less acquainted with. We can get so comfortable at home that we worry more about what strangers think about us, than our own families. The real test comes when we demonstrate our love for God and neighbors, when no one is looking, when no one will know what we have done, said, or thought, no one except for God.

We have to spend time with our church family if we are going to grow in love and demonstrate our love for our fellow believers. That brings up the subject of time. How do we find or make the time for love in action? Love God, love your neighbor as yourself. These are the two greatest commandments, so if I do not have time for loving God and neighbor, then I am spending too much time and effort on the wrong things.

Loving people has lost its priority, lost it importance, lost its emphasis, its appeal. If I felt even a tenth of the love I feel for my own children, for all of God's children, and for all the lost children looking for meaning in life, my life would completely change. I think it is wonderful that when I think of my grandmother, the first thing that comes to mind is how much she loved my dad.

How do I teach the legacy of love to my children? I need to teach and model reading and meditating on the Bible, teach and model talking to God, and teach and model love in action toward our closest and farthest neighbors. As a parent I can be aware of how I use the word love so that I communicate accurately to my children what love is all about. I used to think it was a big subject, but I am starting to think it is as simple as love God, love people (and that is really not simple at all).

My Love Outline

Who
- God
- People

How
- Holy Spirit's help
- Read his Word
- Pray without ceasing to God for all people
- In action

Where
- home, church, family, work, neighborhood, the world, everywhere

When
- all the time

What
- serve one Master, make everything else get in line and out of focus
- I Corinthians 13

Why
- God's mercy in saving me
- Gift of eternal life
- It is how God designed me
- His blessings, protection
- He commands me to love
- Fulfilled, meaningful living

No matter what I set out to teach my children about love, the very scary bottom line is that I must model love for them to truly pass this legacy on. In the same way that I just instinctively felt the deep maternal love my grandma had for my dad, I want my children to sense —see, hear, and feel—my love for God and all people.

I think a lot of people go straight to the love chapter, 1 Corinthians 13, when the subject of love comes up. It has become as popular and expected as Pachelbel's Canon and dyed bridesmaid shoes at weddings. First Corinthians 13 is the standard definition of love, but we cannot stop there because Paul wasn't writing the best man's speech, and besides, who needs to hear these verses at the altar when love seems easy? While we need to know how to love, perhaps the biggest lesson and the place to start is who we love.

Legacy Commitment

1. My Grandma Campbell lived simply and humbly.
- I choose to be content and appreciate the many blessings in my life.
- I will not spoil my children. We will count our blessings together
2. My Grandma Campbell had a fierce, loyal love for her son, my dad.
- I love my children and will tell them so and show them every day as many times as possible.
- I will teach my children to love God and people.

Thinking About Our Legacies

When I first started thinking about love, I had no idea it would boil down to the short and not-so-simple concept of loving God first and loving people. I think the world's emphasis is on how we show our love (typically through buying and giving), our need to love ourselves first (which often involves a lot of buying and giving), and the many things we love. When I looked at Scripture, I found I needed to focus on loving God and people as the legacy I want to pass onto my children.

As with the legacy of faith, it was a helpful exercise for me to spend time defining these colossal concepts to determine how I could make them a part of my life and my children's lives. Take the time to make a list of the things you like, and a list of the people you love, with God at the top. This helps to put things in perspective. My list of people I love, as God has commanded me to, should keep getting longer and longer. My list of things I like is probably already long enough.

Legacy Scripture Verses to Commit to Memory

Do not store up for yourselves treasures on earth, where moth and rust destroy, and where thieves break in and steal. But store up for yourselves treasures in heaven, where moth and rust do not destroy, and where thieves do not break in and steal. For where you treasure is, there you heart will be also. (Matthew 6:19-21 NIV)

But godliness with contentment is great gain. For we brought nothing into the world, and we can take nothing out of it. But if we have food and clothing, we will be content with that. People who want to get rich fall into temptation and a trap and into many foolish and harmful desires that plunge men into ruin and destruction. For the love of money is a root of all kinds of evil. Some people, eager for money, have wandered from the faith and pierced themselves with many griefs. But you, man of God, flee from all this and pursue righteousness, godliness, faith, love, endurance and gentleness. (1 Timothy 6:6-11 NIV)

"Keep your lives free from the love of money and be content with what you have, because God has said, 'Never will I leave you; never will I forsake you'" (Hebrews 13:5 NIV).

"Then He said to them, 'Watch out! Be on your guard against all kinds of greed; a man's life does not consist in the abundance of his possessions"' (Luke 12:15 NIV).

"Behold, what manner of love the Father hath bestowed upon us, that we should be called the sons of God: therefore the world knoweth us not, because it knew him not" (1 John 3:1 KJV). This has been my favorite verse for as long as I can remember, and I first learned it in the KJV, so that is what I prefer for it.

"Dear children, let us not love with words or tongue but with actions and in truth" (1 John 3:18 NIV).

Love is patient, love is kind. It does not envy, it does not boast, it is not proud. It is not self-seeking, it is not easily angered, and it keeps no record of wrongs. Love does not delight in evil but rejoices with the truth. It always protects, always trusts, always hopes, and always perseveres. Love never fails. (1 Corinthians 13:4-8 NIV)

Do not love the world or the things in the world. If anyone loves the world, the love of the Father is not in him. For all that is in the world—the desires of the flesh and the desires of the eyes and pride of life—is not from the Father but is from the world. And the world is passing away along with its desires, but whoever does the will of God abides forever. (1 John 2:15-17 ESV)

See Also
Matthew 22:37-39
John 15:9-17
Romans 8:37-39
John 3:16
I John 4:16
Psalm 52:8b
Proverbs 27:2
Psalm 37:7
Psalm 23

Chapter 5

My Sister, Holly: Discipline and Adventure

I write about each of my siblings in the order of their birth, but that is not absolutely necessary, of course. I can't imagine that siblings would not be included in your journal, but there are no real rules to creating a legacy journal. You will find in this section that I do not pretend to have yet fully captured all of these legacies. That is why I like the word "journey." There is also nothing wrong with dreaming, like when I list expensive vacations.

We went to Myrtle Beach, South Carolina for many years in the fall when my dad had his vacation. We would get out homework from school and do most of it on the ride there. We would spend every day swimming and laying out in the sun. Sometimes we would play mini-golf. Chuck and Becky especially liked the wax museums, which I found just plain creepy.

My dad loves the Adirondack's. We used to go to Old Forge every summer. We would hike up Bald Mountain, and climb the ranger tower at the top whenever it was open. For years you could go to the dump and watch the black bears eat, but at some point they stopped that. (I can't imagine why.) I always liked the quiet serenity of the mountains. It's a great place to read, and maybe that's one reason my dad liked it so much. We would go into town and look through the shops, though we never really bought much there. It was fun to see what they had at the Hardware Store. A special treat was pancakes at Key's Pancake House. The pancakes and maple syrup always tasted better there than anywhere else I have ever had them. There was often a line out the door. At least one morning we would get homemade donuts from a little donut shop that was the best. We swam in the freezing cold lake. Chuck, Becky, and

Holly liked to race swimming across the lake, something I never even tried. Once when we were older, Holly, Becky, and I went for a swim. I turned around and came back when I was tired, thinking about having to make the trip back. Pretty soon after I reached the beach, I hear Becky come walking up behind me. She had climbed in a boat with some strangers when she got too tired and they had brought her to shore.

Becky used to wash her hair in the lake, though I don't really know why. I remember once she washed her hair on the deck when it was raining hard. I think she thought it would be good for her hair. It seems like Holly might have done that too.

I think it was my dad's 60th birthday that I spent with him in Old Forge. We went horseback riding, and somewhere there's a picture of us. We climbed Bald Mountain together on that trip too. I don't think my mom went with us then, because she did not like the mountains. For years we stayed in a beautiful house that had three floors, with multiple bathrooms and decks. It wasn't exactly roughing it, and I have never developed a liking for true camping. My family had a camper that we stayed in at Montrose Bible Conference and in Old Forge, but what I remember most fondly was sleeping in it when it was parked in our driveway. Nothing beats the stars when you are in the Adirondack's. I love the smell of pine and campfires. My parents' friends had a trailer in Old Forge, and many times we rented a cottage at the same campsite. We would stay up late playing Uno and then walk home in the dark (which is darker than town dark).

I particularly remember going out to eat with Becky and Chuck. We always joked about how slow Chuck ate, which he was quite proud of, as he liked to remind us it is good to eat slowly and enjoy your food. Well, we were at this place forever, and as it got cold at night, Chuck put on a baby blue sweater, one of the extras the restaurant had on hand for just such an occasion. It was so funny to us to see him sitting there in a woman's sweater, slowly chewing his steak.

I do not remember how old I was, but when I was very young (I'm sure), I was very upset about the graffiti on the bathroom walls at the campsite. So, I wrote "do not write on the walls" on every single bathroom stall, much to the great amusement of everyone, but mostly Becky.

My sister, Holly, is 8 years older than me, so she helped raise me. I always looked up to her, as far back as I can remember. When she sets her mind to something, she accomplishes it. Holly is tough to beat for discipline and organization. She might not agree, because no one can be perfect at everything, and I'm sure she would point out her weaknesses if we brought up discipline, planning, and organization. Discipline isn't everything, but it sure is at the heart of so much of our lives' goals and dreams. I often hear people joke about their lack of self-discipline when it comes to food, money, household tasks, and getting all sorts of work done. No one brags about their self-discipline, I suppose because they have disciplined their tongues. I believe that one of the most important character traits we can cultivate in ourselves is discipline. It can help you achieve your life's most earnest goals.

Once Holly and her friend Meri-K filled our little pool with Joy dish soap and had the biggest bubble bath you have ever seen. Holly was good at coming up with clever ideas like that. We would go to Montrose Bible Conference during the summer, and there would be a lot of time to kill during the day before the evening service. I remember filling these little paper cups that were in the bathrooms with Kool-Aid, and eating sour crab apples for a snack by the gravestone of the camp founder. It sounds pretty ridiculous now that I'm seeing it in print, but we had a great time. I didn't really like camp, but Holly loved it and even worked there when she got older.

I remember seeing Holly with a small notebook in which she would write down every purchase. No one really wants to budget, I guess, but it sure beats living in debt. When I started college, Holly would send me a check every month. I felt very special to her. She didn't have to do this, of course. It was very sweet and totally unexpected. During any visit to Holly or from Holly, she is likely to bring a gift bag of special items she knows each person will like.

Discipline

Discipline…it's like the pot of gold at the end of the rainbow. Every day I ask God for discipline over my words, my thoughts, food, and money. Then I ask God to keep me from temptation, kind of like a back-up plan for my lack of discipline. I know that if I can lose weight, live on a budget, not say half the stupid things that cross my mind, and keep a positive attitude, surely God is alive and working in me, answering my prayers, and remaking me. When I am apart from the Holy Spirit, I have not been the most disciplined person.

Raising kids is hard work, and discipline is a big part of it. Moms and dads working full-time jobs and raising kids does not make life any easier. This leads me to the next step in my daily prayer. I ask God for energy. The lazy way is much easier in the moment than the disciplined way.

A long train of words comes to mind when I consider discipline: energy, wisdom, accountability, consistency, caring, priorities, decisions, habits, daily. The same way that laziness develops bad habits in me, discipline builds good habits. Every day, and some days are harder than others, I have multiple opportunities to make choices that can benefit me or hurt me. I have to remember to talk to God throughout the day for guidance with all these decisions, for on my own I often make the wrong choice in the moment.

While it is hard to think of my sister lacking discipline in any area, it seems that we all struggle with discipline in different areas and at different times in our lives. I don't know yet where or when my girls will need support in growing discipline in their lives, but even at their young ages I need to be on the lookout for opportunities to purposefully teach them about discipline.

I want to start talking to them now about discipline and all of its offshoots. Maybe if we call a bad habit for what it is, and praise all the good habits, we can teach our children the importance of building discipline into their lives.

I admit I fondly recall the days when my youngest was a newborn (read "baby who still sleeps a lot"), and I would come home from work, settle on the couch with some chocolate and a good book for a relaxing evening (while my husband went to work). Those were short-lived days, and a part of me realizes I shouldn't be proud of taking my sweet time losing extra baby weight, over-eating, and some less than ideal snack choices. I won't apologize for relaxing and holding my babies during nap time. Anyway, I digress. My point here was that very quickly, my kiddos are going to want whatever I am snacking on, and A. it's not part of a balanced diet for growing bodies (which are actually supposed to be growing as opposed to my postpartum body), B. you really need to be 21 or older before you can be trusted to snack neatly on an uneven couch, and C. it's now embarrassing to have eyewitnesses to anything even remotely approaching what could be called pigging out. I am modeling a legacy for my children, right down to my food choices.

It is very important to me that my girls do not have to experience the pain of being obese or overweight. I am the one who brings the food into the house, drives the van through the drive-through, plans the menus, and says yes to going to the playground, so I feel responsible if my children become overweight. I want my girls and me to find our fulfillment in Jesus, not food. We Americans mistreat food and we mistreat our bodies. We don't call it a sin to overeat. It's not illegal. When I don't have the energy to play with my kids because I am carrying around extra weight, I am just sick about it. When I eat because I feel stressed out, instead of relying on God, I am sinning.

It's crunch time. I have two beautiful girls watching my every step. I choose to model, teach, and grow discipline in my household, with God's help. At this point in my legacy journey, I have decided to purchase some index cards on a ring to help with maturing these legacies in my life. I am going to write Bible verses on the cards to carry with me at all times, or at least have within reach. Instead of turning to food, instead of letting negative thoughts linger in my mind, instead of saying words I'll regret, instead of all the countless big and little things I do that speak of laziness and bad habits, I can turn to my Scripture cards and meditate on verses on discipline.

In 1 Timothy 4:7, we are told to discipline ourselves "for the purpose of godliness" (NASB). Physical health is important, or course, but who stops to think of godliness as requiring discipline? Certainly, this journey through the spiritual legacies I want to see evidenced in my life, and that I want to pass onto my children, makes it easy for me to see how discipline for the purpose of godliness is going to be critical.

Adventure

One of the neatest things about Holly is her sense of adventure. Out of curiosity I searched around on the internet to come up with this gem: car seats became mandatory in New York State in 1982. Tennessee was the first state to require car seats in 1978; by 1988 all states had a car seat law. Needless to say, I am from the pre-car seat generation. No wonder my parents thought nothing of throwing us in the station wagon for a trip to Myrtle Beach, South Carolina. The best seat, of course, was the farthest back in the wagon where you could lie down with a book and a blanket. My dad and Jeni's dad had pickup trucks, and we also dangerously enjoyed riding in the bed of the trucks. I'm not sure what the law is on that one, but it's probably a good idea to have one against it. On one particularly memorable trip to South Carolina, with the luggage strapped on top of the car, we had a suitcase casualty when one went flying off during the night never to be seen again. Unfortunately, it was Lori's suitcase, my friend Jeni's older sister who was on vacation with us. I think we all still feel bad about that one.

I took some wonderful trips with Holly, her husband Andy, and their children, Andrew and Elizabeth. As a single adult, I would never have had these opportunities, if Holly hadn't invited me and included me in her family vacations. We went to Florida, Arizona, the Pokinos, and California.

I love Holly's sense of adventure. She's known for planning her next trip while she's on a fabulous vacation. She likes to try new things on the menu at a new restaurant. She taught me that life is an adventure. Also, don't be afraid to try new things, experience life in all its variety. I think it's good to see the world and then go back home where you have loved ones. Take lots of pictures, go lots of places, and see lots of things.

I have never been a skiing, mountain-climbing, thrill-seeking adventurer. But there are all kinds of adventures in life, and I have pursued some, mostly in the form of education. I recently heard someone in my church refer to shyness as a result of pride. I hadn't thought about it like this before, but I can see how a fear of being embarrassed or failing can prevent us from being outgoing or stepping out and trying something new where we will meet new people. Some adventures are people adventures. I am reminded of my grandmother's legacy of love, and God's command to me to love my neighbor as myself. Loving people can certainly be an adventure. It is considerably less trouble to stay home, to keep to myself, and to not ask questions, but how can I love my neighbor without some adventure on my part?

Some adventures are about hard work, which can be pretty tempting to avoid. It is far easier to stay in the town you know, with the friends you trust, and the job you rely on, than to step out in faith when you hear God calling you in a new direction. The apostle Paul wasn't lazy, there's no getting around that. I need to cultivate physical and spiritual discipline so that I can be ready with the energy and spiritual maturity I need when God brings new adventures into my life.

Of course, not all adventures are created equal, and some adventurers might be at risk for carrying their thrill-seeking too far. I picked up and moved five times after high school. That's two colleges, a year and a half in-between, graduate school, and then a doctoral program. Between moves three and four, an older woman I worked with said something that stayed with me through the years, "you need to put down roots at some point." Maybe that doesn't sound so profound to others, but I honestly hadn't considered it before, and it struck a chord with me (though it would still be several years before I did settle down). One of the problems with picking up and moving all the time is that it can make getting married and starting a family a little tricky. Adventure can be wonderful, but there are some really great things about stability, routine, and familiarity.

Early in my doctoral training I remember leaving the library at night, the snow was falling, and the campus was quiet. I thought to myself, "I can't believe I am getting a doctorate." It just hit me in that moment, and I admit, it felt great. School has been an adventure, and I am glad I pursued my education. Of course I want the best for my daughters, but having earned a PhD, I can honestly say it is not what defines me, it is not my greatest achievement, and it is not what makes me happy. I want my girls to go for their dreams, but more than anything, I want them to make becoming like Christ their number one goal.

One of my favorite adventures was a two-week trip to London and Paris with my best friend, Jenniffer when we were in our early twenties. As a parent now, it is scary to think about my girls even hearing that we set out for Europe alone as young women. We had always said we wanted to go, and so we did. My husband and I had both always wanted to experience Italy, so when it came time to plan our honeymoon, Italy it was. I always wanted to write a book, and now I am. I love the idea of teaching my children to dream big, plan, and then do it.

For fun I planned the next 15 years of family vacations. My husband looked scared when he saw the list. I did not bother to get out my calculator and estimate how much it is going to cost us, and it might very well not be possible to include all these destinations. This activity did make me think about when would be the best time to visit places, based on things like family graduations and school curriculums. I listed the years with my children's ages. It is a pretty outrageous list, and I think I'll just keep it tucked away somewhere so as not to overwhelm anyone. On second thought, why not...

Disney World (addicting)
Disney Cruise (I am already rethinking this one, because $1,000/ night seems, well, ridiculous)
Creation Museum in Petersburg, KY
Boston, MA
Philadelphia, PA
Williamsburg, PA
Washington, D.C.
New York City
San Diego, CA and the Redwoods
Grand Canyon
Yellowstone National Park
Alaska
Europe (probably not all of it)
Hawaii
Venice

The greatest adventure of all is our journey toward becoming like Christ. The next greatest adventure in line for me, and I think my husband would agree, is raising children. As I pursue Christ-likeness, I desperately want to inspire my children to pursue Christ-likeness.

Adventure Stoppers:	Adventure Boosts:
• fear • pride • laziness	• energy • listening to God's guidance • be open, "here am I, send me" • dream big • trust God

Legacy Commitment

1. My sister is a disciplined, goal-oriented person.
- I will set goals and discipline myself to meet those goals.
- I will help my children to set goals and reach their goals.
2. I admire my sister's sense of adventure and love of travel.
- I will not be afraid of trying new things, doing new things, or going new places.
- I will share adventure and travel with my children.

Thinking About Our Legacies

Children love adventures. Just look at all the movies and television shows they like. Make a list of the adventures you want to commit to experiencing with your children. Are there certain places you definitely want to go as a family? Trips are expensive and, as everyone says, the years go by quickly. What other kinds of adventures do you want to have with your children? Could you sponsor or support a child in need? Do you want to learn how to sew, ice skate, or make a great pie crust with them? There are a lot of classes and clubs out there for kids, but what about adventures you could take as a family? Taking the time to think about and plan for these things will increase the likelihood of them happening, and help organize your ideas.

Legacy Scripture Verses to Commit to Memory

"For the Spirit God gave us does not make us timid, but gives us power, love and self-discipline" (2 Timothy 1:7 NIV).

For the grace of God has appeared that offers salvation to all people. It teaches us to say "No" to ungodliness and worldly passions, and to live self-controlled, upright and godly lives in this present age, while we wait for the blessed hope—the appearing of the glory of our great God and Savior, Jesus Christ, who gave himself for us to redeem us from all wickedness and to purify for himself a people that are his very own, eager to do what is good. (Titus 2:11-14 NIV)

"No temptation has overtaken you except what is common to mankind. And God is faithful; he will not let you be tempted beyond what you can bear. But when you are tempted, he will also provide a way out so that you can endure it" (1 Corinthians 10:13 NIV).

The next passage caused a light bulb to go off for me, when I considered that I must "make every effort" to incorporate these character traits in my life. It is tempting to pray about it and then sit back and wait for God to change me, but these verses seem to indicate that I have a very active part in pursuing self-control and godliness, as well as the other qualities mentioned here.

His divine power has given us everything we need for a godly life through our knowledge of him who called us by his own glory and goodness. Through these he has given us his very great and precious promises, so that through them you may participate in the divine nature, having escaped the corruption in the world caused by evil desires.

For this very reason, make every effort to add to your faith goodness; and to goodness, knowledge; and to knowledge, self-control; and to self-control, perseverance; and to perseverance, godliness; and to godliness, mutual affection; and to mutual affection, love. For if you possess these qualities in increasing measure, they will keep you from being ineffective and unproductive in your knowledge of our Lord Jesus Christ. (2 Peter 1:3-8 NIV)

"Good sense makes one slow to anger, and it is his glory to overlook an offense" (Proverbs 19:11 ESV).

Have nothing to do with irreverent, silly myths. Rather train yourself for godliness; for while bodily training is of some value, godliness is of value in every way, as it holds promise for the present life and also for the life to come. The saying is trustworthy and deserving of full acceptance. For to this end we toil and strive, because we have our hope set on the living God, who is the Savior of all people, especially of those who believe.

Command and teach these things. (1 Timothy 4:7-11 ESV)

See Also
Proverbs 13:3
Proverbs 21:20
1 Thessalonians 4:4

Chapter 6

My Brother, Chuck: Work and Visit

For some people it was easier than others to come up with the legacies I felt I could learn from them. Once I had settled on qualities, they seemed obvious to me. There is admittedly some overlap, like visiting and being friendly. I see my brother visiting, and my sister being friendly with everyone, as separate legacies. Did I mention that there are no rules? Perhaps you have the same legacy from more than one person. Write what makes sense for you.

Work

My brother, Chuck, is seven years older than me. He is a hard worker, and I think he enjoys working too. The American dream was originally built on a strong work ethic. People believed if you worked hard enough, you could achieve your highest ambitions. Sometimes it seems like people feel entitled to a big house, better than the one he or she grew up in, with all kinds of luxuries, and no one wants to work long and hard to get it. God expects us to work hard six days a week, and He promises to provide for our needs. If you work hard for what you have, you will appreciate it more, and you will have the satisfaction of your accomplishments.

It is one of my greatest desires for my children that they find meaningful work they love. We cleaned the house growing up, and we all had jobs as soon as we were able to work. I used to babysit all the kids on our street. When I turned 16 I worked in a grocery store.

My dad grew up on a farm. I think he was always used to hard work. He held various jobs, including being a pastor, baggage handler for Greyhound bus, working in the laundry room of a hospital, and working as a general contractor. He was always up early with a cup of coffee and his Bible.

My brother has also always been a hard worker. He had a paper route when he was in high school, and has worked hard at various jobs since, including roofing. I vaguely recall that there used to be a morning and evening edition of the newspaper. Chuck has never carried an ounce of fat, and while some of that may be thanks to a great metabolism, I think a lot of it has to do with hard work.

It is easy and tempting to be lazy in life today. Television shows rarely depict adults working hard, even if they are at the office. Instead we see beautiful adults sitting around drinking coffee, shopping, or just hanging out in designer clothes in their large Manhattan flats. Okay, I don't watch that much TV (if you don't count Veggie Tales), but my suspicion is that a lot of TV shows and movies convey a carefree, fun, glamorous lifestyle where the good life comes naturally and quickly. The reality for most of us isn't as television worthy. Budgeting, hard work, patience, discipline—these are our true daily efforts. I think we are all at risk for feeling entitled to more, to better, to easier. At the same time, we may not want to work harder for all that we want. The hard truth is that we need to work hard to succeed in our jobs day after day.

Hard work is required of us in more places than on the job. I just heard a quote that really speaks to this: "it is hard to lose weight, hard to keep weight off, and hard to be overweight. Choose your hard." This is a good reminder for me in all my complaining about how hard losing weight is. Being overweight is hard too! All the get-thin-quick weight-loss products and pills are just a lie, preying on our refusal to work hard and steadfastly.

We work hard in our homes in countless says, so it can be difficult to see how we are supposed to have it so much easier nowadays. I do think about how simple it is to throw dirty clothes in two machines, and pull out clean laundry. There is no denying this household task has gotten easier through the years. We work hard in marriage, family, and church, to name just a few areas well worth our hard work. If I am going to be doing all this hard work, I had better set some goals and prioritize so I know what I am exerting all this effort for.

I have tried at least three times that I can recall to keep a mother's journal. I have not lasted very long in these previous endeavors. This time is different. I am engaging on a journey in a sense, writing my own childhood journal that I can share with my children. I am able to keep inspired, moving ahead, and working hard because I can see the value for me, for my children, and for any readers who might stumble upon my legacy journey. This time writing has become the easy part. The hard work is coming to terms with all the ways I want to change to be the person I believe God created me to be. Did God put all of these people in my life to teach me these lessons of faith, love, discipline, and so forth? The first step in this journey is the meditation on who I am, who I could be, and who my children can be. Then begins the journey of establishing these legacies in my life and the lives of my children. I am thankful I don't have to do it alone, or by my own efforts, but together with my husband, with the Holy Spirit working in our lives.

Visiting

Chuck likes talking to people. One of the great joys in life is a good conversation with someone. Nowadays, it seems everyone has his or her head buried in a smart phone. The most important thing in the world is the people in the world. Talk to people, hear their stories, listen to their hearts. When I moved to Rochester, Chuck helped me, and I remember him giving me a couple rolls of dimes he had, which came in handy as I started out in a new town with a new job, and money was tight. My mom likes to tell how Chuck would take me out of the crib as soon as he got home from school. Those little memories are sweet and fun for me to think about.

If you have "visited" Victorian England through the books of Jane Austen or Charles Dickens, you are acquainted with the customs of "at home days," "visiting cards," and "paying calls." I suppose you could argue that these 19th century ladies did not have the benefit of phones, texting, emailing, and Facebook, and that ladies did not work outside the home, and had servants. These are valid points, but the custom of visiting, with no other purpose, does seem long gone. It is a quaint concept from a bygone era, though I won't deny that it probably involved gossip and prejudice. These visits never seemed long in books or movies, but they did seem like an important part of their lives.

I wish we took the time and effort to visit, and not just at Christmas.

My brother is an expert in the art of visiting and asking questions, sharing stories, never rushing, pausing, being together, sitting, and just being a part of each other's lives. I need to take the time and exercise the patience needed to visit with family, friends, my church family, coworkers, neighbors, acquaintances, and strangers. Practice makes perfect.

I don't want to overlook the significance of visiting with my own family. People joke about how when asked about their day kids do "nothing" at school, and spouses do "nothing" at work. Visiting takes practice, and I want to be sure and model visiting with my husband for my children to see. We tell people they are important, they matter to us, when we take the time to visit. I certainly want my children to know how important they are to me. Who knows, maybe someday, when I ask what they did at school, they'll sit and chat with me about teachers, lessons, friends, and playground fun, instead of mumbling "nothing." I want my children to know they have my attention.

Visiting is an investment in other people, and it can be an investment in ourselves as well. You just never know when someone unexpected will share something we really need to hear. It could be news of a job opening, a much-needed parenting tip, or words of encouragement that lifts our soul.

Legacy Commitment

1. I respect my brother's strong work ethic.
- I will work hard at everything I do.
- I will teach my children to work hard in all their tasks.
2. My brother gets out and talks to people.
- I will take the time to sit and listen, and talk and share with others.
- I will be a good listener for my children, and provide them with opportunities to talk with lots of different kinds of people.

Thinking About Our Legacies

I am a big believer in the power of words. When I think about teaching my children the art of visiting, I like the idea of incorporating the use of the word "visiting" into my children's lives. I'll say, "let's visit. Tell me what you did today while I was at work." I get all the good, the bad, and the ugly news this way, which my oldest daughter relishes sharing with me. My children hear me visiting on the phone with my family and friends, so I want to point out to them I plan to spend more time visiting with them than others. Have you ever thought about having a planned visiting time with your family? For some people this is over dinner, but with little kids dinner can be a big chore that doesn't lend itself well to visiting. Sometimes I visit with my children while they take their baths, or before bed. Of course, we can't forget to visit with our spouses! After our families comes all kinds of opportunities for short and long visits with our friends, church family, neighbors, and strangers.

Have you noticed how often people repeat themselves? Maybe I am doing it too, but I am surprised at how often someone will tell me something they have already told me. Personally, I just listen again because what is the point in stopping someone when clearly they need someone to talk to. People desperately need people to listen, really listen to them. I don't need to come up with answers, solutions, wise words, or pithy quotes. If I just actively listen, I have responded to their need.

Legacy Scripture to Commit to Memory

"Whatever you do, work at it with all your heart, as working for the Lord, not for human masters, since you know that you will receive an inheritance from the Lord as a reward. It is the Lord Christ you are serving" (Colossians 3:23-24 NIV).

Chapter 7

My Sister, Becky: Friendliness and Giving

Ah, Becky. We fought, disagreed, and argued with each other for years. Then, magically we turned into best friends. I like to tell my girls they are best friends, that they'll always have each other, and other equally sentimental things. One of the benefits of putting your legacy journey on paper is that it helps you to appreciate what you have. Don't be afraid to get sentimental and mushy.

My sister, Becky, is one of the most outgoing, friendliest people I know. This is no exaggeration. Becky is four years older than me. We didn't always get along as kids, but that didn't mean anyone else was allowed to be mean to me. We shared a room sometimes. She was very messy. We had a line down the middle of the room for our separate sides. We spent a lot of time playing board games, including Monopoly, Pay Day, Careers, UNO, Skip Bo, Parcheesi, Life, Trouble, Candy Land, Chutes and Ladders, Sorry, checkers, and our personal favorite, Clue. The computer and Internet were not entertaining us back then, so we had to settle for playing red light, green light; hide-and-go-seek; and hop scotch. When we ventured inside to watch TV, it was Flintstones, The Jetsons, Loony Tunes, and later Silver Spoons, Family Ties, The Facts of Life, and Growing Pains. There was a long list of shows we were not allowed to watch, including Dallas, Fantasy Island, and soap operas. We always looked forward to the Christmas movies, and we would closely examine the TV Guide for when the shows would be on. It doesn't seem as special now when you can pull up a movie on Netflix whenever you want.

I want my children to remember me as being happy. My sisters and I loved watching Little House on the Prairie. Becky and I absolutely adored the main character Laura. I don't remember "Ma," Caroline, typically having a central role in the episodes, but when I think of her, I see her smiling and laughing. Now when I watch the show, the episodes seems very sad and depressing, and I can't understand how it didn't bother me as a child. I remember talking about this to my sister, Becky, when we were older, and we had a good laugh when we both commented on the single episode we could remember that was not sad. That would be the Halloween episode, in case you are wondering, and to be honest, it wasn't the best Little House episode. So, even through all those hard times, Ma kept on smiling and laughing. I know it is just a show, but I can't exaggerate how big a show it was in our lives growing up. I want to make sure my children see me smiling and laughing a lot, and I mean a lot. When they look back on their childhoods and think of mom, I want them to get a picture in their minds of me smiling and laughing.

When I got older, and after Becky moved to Florida, we started to get along a whole lot better. I hope that my girls will get along right from the start and throughout their whole lives. It is very special to have a sister, because unfortunately, sometimes friends lose touch and move in and out of each others' lives, but a sister is for life. I know that is a cliché, but for the most part it's true. I went to Florida to visit Becky and her family a couple of times. Becky and her girls, Victoria and Isabel, and I went to Disney World and had the time of our lives.

Becky is not afraid to talk to anyone. I remember Halloween being fun with her. My friend Jeni and I would trick-or-treat together, and some years, Becky went with us as well. What else do I want my kids to know about their Aunt Becky? She would lay out in the sun all day long, even putting Crisco on to try and get tanner. We didn't know much about the need to protect skin from the sun back then. Becky loves to exercise, and even jokes that no one wants to be around her if she hasn't gone for a run. She has always been able to eat as much as she wants. I remember even when we were little, she could eat a Big Mac, fries, and a soft drink. She'll order an appetizer, meal, and dessert. She is so much fun to be around. Sometimes I just roll my eyes when she starts talking to strangers, but I have to admit, it is fun.

Friendliness

There are people we want to be friendly toward, those we feel we have to be friendly toward, and then there might be people we do not want to be friendly with, or some we do not even notice enough to be friendly toward.

Becky knows the names of the employees at the grocery store she shops at. No joke. She knows everyone's names in her neighborhood. She knows the teachers, the students, the other parents from her children's school. I feel we honor people when we remember and use their names. I show you are important to me when I call you by name. Who hasn't had the experience of someone unexpectedly using your name in a greeting? It feels surprising and good. I feel important in that moment, and then humbled if I don't remember that person's name. It has become perfectly acceptable to lament, "I'm not good with names," but I suspect that's just a way to excuse laziness, lack of concern, and lack of attention. Paying attention to people's names and using them is a good place for me to start on a path toward friendliness.

My sister has a well-established reputation for friendliness that even her children live in awe and fear of. Becky invited me on a trip to Disney World with her and her children before I was married, and her husband had to work. We were relaxing in our hotel room after a non-stop day at the park. I had been sitting on the balcony; there was a couple on the balcony next door, also enjoying the cool evening and giraffes at the amazing Animal Park hotel. I may have said hello to this couple. I don't remember, but it wasn't more than a polite, quick greeting, if anything. I stepped inside to use the bathroom, and by the time I came back out, Becky was deep in conversation with this couple from Australia, as if they had known each other for years. I could go on and on with story after story like this.

My husband is very friendly too. When we were house hunting, I thought we could visit some open houses. I mapped out a few open houses with their addresses and times, and set out with my plan for the day with my husband. I hadn't figured my husband's outgoing personality into my plan. We only made it to one open house because Luke was visiting with the realtor about sports, the town, and other topics. On my own going to open houses, I said as little to the realtors as possible, and could fit in four or even five in a day. I had to take house hunting into my own hands after that, or we might still be out there visiting with realtors. Even though I joke about it, I do enjoy quite a few of the conversations started by my husband and my sister with perfect strangers. The truth is you just never know how your life or another person's life might be enriched when we are friendly.

Obviously, being friendly is similar to visiting, but it brings up a point I've encountered before. There are people in our inner circle, our family and closest friends, and then there are acquaintances and strangers. Sometimes taking time to visit and be friendly with our inner circle can be taken for granted, while we are more hesitant to offend acquaintances or strangers. This is unreasonable, and something I feel I need to be on guard against.

I can make a plan and set aside time for visiting. Being friendly is an attitude I want to adopt on a daily basis. Needless to say, sometimes it is easier than others to be friendly. When I'm tired, in a hurry, or just not in a good mood, my store of friendliness starts to get depleted quickly. As a teenager I worked in a grocery store, so I appreciate the tedious, mind-numbing task of scanning boxes and cans, punching keys, sorting through coupons, and bagging others' purchases. I'm sensitive to the long hours, short breaks, and hearing your name impatiently called over the loudspeaker to the front of the store. So I try to be friendly when I am in line at the store, and I definitely work to not be rude even if something rings up wrong, the customer in front of the line runs back for a forgotten item, my gallon of milk is leaking, or something just won't scan. (I have a knack for selecting the one item on the shelf without a scanning code.) World peace isn't at stake here. I can stay friendly for a few minutes and make the cashier's job a little easier, a lot less annoying.

It is nice to go somewhere with friendly people because I know I can relax and enjoy myself. This is because I know my friendly husband is going to help put people at ease. Making others comfortable is another great reason to be friendly. If I am rejoicing in the Lord always, some of that joy should be spreading over to people I come in contact with. Isn't that a great feeling when a friendly encounter leaves you smiling, content, just happy in the moment—a moment that can change and direct the course of your day.

Some have argued that being outgoing is a personality trait. The "people person" versus the "task person" explanation can be an excuse. I can choose to be friendly. It doesn't mean I have to throw a party every weekend. We spend so much time and effort studying why people are the way they are. Nature versus nurture, the role of genetics and environment, experts weighing in on their research finds. God, our Creator, can change us. He is not held captive by our strong personality traits, our backgrounds, or even our past poor choices or behavior. A nice reminder of this is found in Philippians 1:6: "being confident of this, that he who began a good work in you will carry it on to completion until the day of Christ Jesus" (NIV).

I didn't realize how important being friendly is to me until I started exploring my sister's legacy of friendliness. People like to say hi to kids. They try to get the high five, a wave, at least a smile. A couple of times my three year old has explained to me that she is shy when I ask her why she didn't say hi to someone. I don't like to hear this excuse coming from her because I know she must have heard it from me and my husband regarding her. A child's smile, handshake, or little high five can brighten a person's day in a special way, and I hate to think that her dismissal of others has caused any hurt or embarrassment, however small it might be, and that she has missed an opportunity to bring joy to another person. So we have begun practicing the art of friendliness. I'm not asking her to tap dance on tables for my friends, just wave, smile, and the big achievements—say hello and goodbye, with an occasional high five or fist bump. Which reminds me, I need to model friendliness for my children to become comfortable with it.

Giving

Becky is a giving person, which strikes me as a special, unique thing to say about a person. I've had the pleasure of taking a few trips with my sister, and she took good care of me. Becky will say things like "if I won the lottery, I would buy this for _____, and do this for _____." She thinks about all the special treats she can have on hand for guests. You can tell she likes playing Santa Claus at Christmas time, and boy does she love Christmas.

Gary Chapman, author and pastor, believes that people feel loved when you speak their love language: words of affirmation, quality time, receiving gifts, acts of service, or physical touch. I don't believe receiving gifts is my love language, but knowing that it can be for some people is a good reminder to be generous. I would like to cover my bases, so to speak, and be fluent in all the love languages.

I live giving gifts, but honestly sometimes it hurts a little financially, and I have to continually remind myself to give back to God first. It is easier to give when you get to experience the receiver's thanks and appreciation for your thoughtfulness and generosity. It feels good. Acknowledging my selfishness makes me want to give anonymously, when it has no specific benefit to me. Then, I can experience the joy of giving, without the sting of selfishness or pride lingering in the back of my mind. Am I giving to impress people, so they will like me? I think these are good questions for me to ask myself when I give.

As a Christian and church member, I give to support the church and the work of God through that church. Again I am aware how my husband and I set the example for our children. I plan to teach my children early to save, tithe, and spend wisely. I haven't been very good about remembering to give my children money for the offering plate for missions in their Sunday School classes, so now I am reminding myself to get going, because the teaching starts now.

Isn't it funny how some people are more fun to give to than others, and it seems the less fun are those who need my gifts more? There are some people I just get, I know what they like, I know what they'll really appreciate, and it feels great to find the perfect gift for them. The trouble is they probably do not need anything, truthfully. On the other hand, I know some, dare I say prickly people, who do have needs, but are just difficult to buy or do for. It is not fun to buy for someone who is never satisfied or openly appreciative. I think the only answer here can be to pray that the Holy Spirit direct me to the right gifts at the right time.

I have read many hair-raising, send a chill down my spine stories of people praying and receiving exactly what they needed when they needed it. I pray God would honor me by using me in such a way. I pray that he will make me into someone He can use as a giver, whether it is gifts, time, the right words, attention, an act of service, or a hug.

Legacy Commitment

1. No one could accuse my sister of being unfriendly.
- I will be friendly, even when I don't feel like it.
- I will actively teach and encourage my children to be friendly and outgoing.
2. Becky is a giving person.
- I choose to be a giving person, when it is easy, and when it is difficult.
- I will teach my children to be giving, to share with each other and with people in need.

Thinking About Our Legacies

We easily think about giving at Christmas time. We make our lists of who to buy for and our gift ideas. This year I plan to brave a store with my children, help them pick out a few gifts for others, set them free with some wrapping paper, tape, and non-breakable gifts, and just see what happens. I am not going to rewrap their gifts (I had to say this to commit to letting it go). I don't think it can be too early to teach them about giving as well as receiving.

Legacy Scripture to Commit to Memory

"Remember this: Whoever sows sparingly will also reap sparingly, and whoever sows generously will also reap generously. Each of you should give what you have decided in your heart to give, not reluctantly or under compulsion, for God loves a cheerful giver" (2 Corinthians 9:6-7 NIV).

"Give to the one who asks you, and do not turn away from the one who wants to borrow from you" (Matthew 5:42 NIV).

"Being confident of this, that he who began a good work in you will carry it on to completion until the day of Christ Jesus" (Philippians 1:6 NIV).

See Also
2 Corinthians 8:1-8

Chapter 8

My Friend, Jenniffer: Kindness and Friendship

There can be little sweeter than a childhood friend. While I focused on my childhood, that does not mean that you have to. Whenever a friend comes along, grab her or him and hold on. Kindness is one of my favorite attributes, and honestly, one I have struggled with throughout my life. On one hand, I am passionate about being kind to hurting people, but at the same time, I can be rude and impatient. It is a journey after all.

Thinking of my childhood friend makes me think about the fashion from our childhood. I don't remember ever being especially fashion-conscious, but I did have my favorite outfits over the years. I would reserve my favorite pair of pants for Friday. After 6th grade I went to a Christian school where I had to wear a dress every day. I adored Anne of Green Gables, in addition to Little House on the Prairie, so I enjoyed wearing dresses anyway. I don't think I gave my mom a hard time when it came to clothes. I had the benefit of watching my older siblings' interactions with my mom, and I think I decided pretty early it was wisest to try to fly under the radar. There was one time I remember, however, where I decided I had to put my foot down. It was an off-white dress with an olive green skirt, a color that was not in vogue at the time, at least to my knowledge. If that wasn't bad enough, this dress had a large, bright orange belt that offended me greatly. I cried and cried all Sunday morning about that dress. When I got to church, one of the greeters who could tell I had been crying asked me what was wrong. I explained my tragic plight, and he offered some, I thought, excellent, wise advice. He suggested I remove the belt, and maybe that would make me feel better. Well, my mom was not very happy with me when she saw I had altered my look. To make matters significantly worse, that afternoon my sister discovered my dress had holes in both underarms, and of course accused me of purposefully making them. I was not that devious, and I defend my honor to this day, but it looked suspicious in light of my day-long temper tantrum over the dress. I did get to wear something else to church that night, which I was still able to enjoy, despite the accusations and unpleasantness of the day.

We wore leg warmers over our jeans. For a while we would roll the bottoms of our jeans as tightly as possible together and then pile bulky, colorful socks over them. We threaded friendship beads onto safety pins and gave them out to each other to wear on our shoes. More than any-thing, our hair provided the greatest canvas of all for expressing our creativity and fastidiousness. We suffered through smelly perms to get our hair as curly as possible. Long hair got the spiral perm treatment. Why straight hair couldn't have been in fashion when I was growing up, I'll never know, but it is truly a shame. Banana clips were a girl's best friend. They really did look good in everyone's hair, or at least we thought so at the time. Of course we teased our bangs to get really good volume. Big, and I really do mean big, very large, hair bows were all the rage. Similar to friendship beads for our shoes, we would make barrettes with colorful ribbons hanging from them for each other. It just doesn't seem like we are as creative with our hair anymore. Jenniffer (her family has a legacy of unusual name spellings) taught me how to French-braid hair, and I think of her when I do my girls' hair.

Jenniffer, who we called Jeni for at least the first 15 years, grew up across the street from me. That's the first and most important thing to know. I don't remember ever not knowing Jeni. My mom likes to tell a story about how I did not like Jeni at first, and would move from one swing set to the other when she came over. I do not remember this, but I was a shy child, so it is possible that I was wary at first, but I assure you Jeni and I were friends from the beginning. My childhood memories are completely enveloped in my friendship with Jeni. I pray that my girls have each other first, and then friendships like the one I enjoyed growing up, and still enjoy.

Kindness

I simply do not recall Jeni ever saying anything mean about anyone at any time. Now, I am sure that cannot be entirely true, but what a legacy! Jeni is nice. Nice might not seem like a big deal. It's a small word, and seems kind of general, but its impact is huge. The Bible says, "And be ye kind one to another, tender-hearted, forgiving one another, even as God for Christ's sake has forgiven you" (Ephesians 4:32 NIV).

Like all kids, I'm sure we had our arguments, not that I can think of any (or would admit to any), but I will say, Jeni never held a grudge. Being kind does not allow for that kind of drawn-out meanness. Jeni and I played together every chance we had. We didn't spend our time talking about other people, or certainly not on computers or phones, which did not make their appearance into our world until later.

One of our favorite things to do was to pack a bag and take a hike to Big Rock. Jeni had a huge backyard that went up and up to a very big hill. This would probably not seem as big today, but it was a big hike back then. There was a large rock that sort of stuck out from the side of this hill, which we named Big Rock. We would sit on Big Rock and have a snack and some Kool-Aid (which we drank by the gallon in the days before Crystal Light). Once, we emptied out our backpacks and took the neighbor's kittens with us, which we pretended were our babies. This caused quite a stir in the neighborhood, because we neglected to tell anyone where we were going, and there was a general feeling that we had been abducted. In our defense, we were always gone together from morning until dark, but for some reason this one time the neighborhood was in a big commotion when we returned from Big Rock. I don't know what part they thought the cats played in all of this. I also don't know why that neighbor always had so many cats.

We would sled down the hills in the winter, outside all day in our big snow suits. Now I am cold if I am outside for more than five minutes. We would come inside to one of our houses and have hot chocolate and a cookie. My mom often baked cookies and other yummy treats. We had all kinds of sleds. I remember Jeni had a big, old fashioned toboggan sleigh that a bunch of people could go on together. We would break off icicles hanging from the house as carefully as possible, trying to keep them long so we could eat them.

We used to "boot skate" which was us pretending to ice skate on a big pond behind our house. A house burned down when I was young, and the foundation hole it left became a pond we fished tadpoles out of in the spring, and an ice skating rink in the winter. Becky had ice skates, but the rest of us just boot-skated, imagining in our minds we looked just like the figure skaters we enjoyed watching on TV. Today I watch my daughters pretend to ice skate, and I am not embarrassed to admit, I pretend right along with them.

Snow-days were the best. Jeni and I had walkie talkies and we would talk to each other as soon as we heard the good news. We would plan whose house to meet at and make breakfast together before heading out all day to play. Of course we would make snowmen and snow angels, eat snow and icicles, go sledding, and then come inside to make Kraft macaroni and cheese for lunch.

We used to put on these shows for our parents where we did gymnastics routines on the walkway beside Jeni's house. I am sure it was the silliest thing ever, but I don't remember anyone making fun of us. Once we put some grapes or berries in water to serve as refreshments, but they fermented before the big show. Becky and Jeni and I used to pick berries all over the neighborhood. We ate as we picked, and I'm not really sure if we ever actually saved enough for a pie, but I think that was our goal. We would ride our bikes up and down the street with no bike helmets, and sometimes pretty poorly functioning brakes. Becky was very proud of her bike with the big banana seat. There is a street next to ours that was the ultimate challenge to ride down. This street was the other side of the big hill we climbed behind Jeni's house. We would ride down it with our legs out and no brakes until the bottom. I was always less adventurous than others in the neighborhood. I don't remember that I even took the bike ride down the whole hill. My sisters would walk across the monkey bars, swing high and jump to grab the hanging rope, and do all kinds of flips and crazy moves on that swing set in our backyard.

Jeni's Grandma Cornish lived in the first floor apartment of her house. She would spray us with the water hose if we rode our bikes in her driveway to turn around. Kids did it on purpose, of course. Behind Jeni's house was a big-roofed porch. We would play games out there, and even spend the night out there sometimes. It was one of the tragic mysteries of our youth that Jeni's grandma wouldn't let the family enclose this space. I don't even remember why it was so important to us, but we would moan and groan about it.

Jeni's backyard was filled with big walnut trees. We would gather the nuts in brown paper bags, the kind you used to get from the grocery store when the clerks would ask if you wanted paper or plastic. Walnuts come in a green outer shell. We would break them open with a hammer and sit on that back porch eating as many as we wanted. Her family grew grapes on trellises on the side of the house. I remember my mom often grew tomatoes, and when I was old enough I had one section of the garden I could use for myself. I remember growing peas in the pod. I don't remember what else I put in there, but I was very proud of my garden.

Jeni's father worked at a landfill. He brought home some treasures, including a green glass coffee table that I think he made himself. By far the greatest find was a large green chalkboard just like the ones they had in school. This chalkboard hung in what we called the "back room" at Jeni's house. We loved to play school, and having a real chalkboard really made our play come alive.

I called Jeni's mom, Mrs. C, and she was very special to me. Later in life, Jeni and her sisters would take care of Mrs. C until they no longer could, and she moved into a nursing home. My memories of Mrs. C are mostly from our childhood, but seeing how her children took such good care of her, is a legacy of its own.

Mrs. C made the best spaghetti with homemade sauce that would simmer all day. She could crochet and knit, and once tried to teach me how to crochet. I wasn't very good, and could really only do straight lines. I suppose I just didn't apply myself. Jeni made some beautiful blankets. Mrs. C made me the Christmas stocking I still use each year, plus the little stockings we hang on the tree. She was good at crafty things, a talent I think Jeni inherited. She would take containers that other people would throw out, and decorate them, making them pretty and special, fun for another use. I have tried to do this as well, and it always brings to mind Mrs. C.

It was common when I was growing up to call all adults Mr. and Mrs. I kind of miss this respect. It always seems awkward for me to tell my girls the names of adults. I don't know if I should use a first name, or a title and last name. It seemed special and fun to me to call Jeni's mom, Mrs. C.

Mrs. C was fun to be around, and the strange thing is, I am not exactly sure why. I guess there is a just a presence and peace that some people possess that makes others want to be close by. It is nice to know people you feel comfortable with, even if you couldn't say why that is if you were asked. I think it comes from making people feel special.

I have always thought of Jeni as one of the nicest people I know. I cannot think that anyone would ever have anything bad to say about her. What a legacy: being nice and caring about others. There are very few (if any) times I have heard her say anything negative about anyone. Of course no one is perfect, but if someone can say that they have a hard time thinking of something negative you have ever said, that is a special thing. This makes me think of Daniel, one of my favorite people in the Bible.

Kindness doesn't even begin to explain Jenniffer carrying her sister's baby for her, after years of childlessness for her older sister. We share the best part of ourselves when we show kindness, and fortunately, it doesn't always have to be this big.

Kind thoughts, words, and actions can be expressed every day. Kindness strikes me as a state of being because there are opportunities almost constantly coming at us and through us to be kind. Kindness, similar to giving, might be most needed where it is most difficult.

If I were to rank my goals for my children, kindness would be among the top contenders. I feel almost desperate for my girls to be kind toward others, and that this be a strong trait in them. It is so easy to hurt hurting people with the wrong words, yet so easy to help people with the right words.

What if I replaced some of the "you are so pretty" comments to my girls, with "you are so kind"? Wouldn't this begin to plant the seed of kindness, to acknowledge what is really important and worthy of praise? I think it's a good start. I'm going to throw the word "kind" around until it catches root in the lives of my girls.

Friendship

A long friendship is a beautiful thing. I love to hear stories of high school sweethearts or friends who met on the first day of kindergarten. I want to make a point of regularly praying for my girls to be best friends, and also to have wonderful friendships with others. Friendship that can grow, blossom, console, comfort, teach, rejoice, and just be with.

God already knows who can be great friends for my girls. I see my job as providing opportunities and exposure, and to model and teach (again with the modeling) good friendship skills. It is easier to stay home on Wednesday evenings after a long day of work, but what my girls and I need (my husband has to work, so this makes it even more of a challenge), is to spend time with our Christian brothers and sisters, to nurture these friendships, by being present consistently, and practicing our friendship skills.

I never really had any true friends in church growing up, and I want to be sensitive to my children to make sure that same pattern isn't repeated. I enjoyed church as a child, but it was still unpleasant to spend so much time in a place without friends. Cliques can form anywhere, and in my youth group, church sides seemed to be divided up as those in public schools and those in Christian school. I went to a Christian school from 7th grade on, and I thoroughly enjoyed it. I could be wrong about the source of the separation of kids at church. It could have been location. We travelled about 25 minutes to church, so we never saw each other outside of church. This same situation is in place now. We live a distance from our church, so I wonder how this will impact our children. I don't want to dwell on negative memories, but I do want to be sensitive to my girls' friendship needs.

Legacy Commitment

1. Jeni is simply put, one of the nicest people I know.
- I will practice kindness every day, and ask forgiveness when I have been unkind.
- I will praise my children for every kindness I see in them, and I will correct any unkindness. I will emphasize the importance of kindness.
2. It takes work to maintain a friendship, and Jeni has been one of the best at it.
- I will be a great friend.
- I will teach my children to be great friends, first to each other, and

then with other worthy friends. I will find opportunities for my girls to make friends. I will pray for their friends.

Thinking About Our Legacies

It is never too late to pray and ask God to give you the gift of a true friend, and it is never too early to pray and ask God to give your children the gift of true friends. Ask your children who their friends are and what they like about these friends. Think about whom you spend time with and where you spend time. This is purposefully planning for who your children will be friends with.

Legacy Scripture Verses to Commit to Memory

"Be kind and compassionate to one another, forgiving each other, just as in Christ God forgave you" (Ephesians 4:32 NIV). I also like how the KJV says to be "tenderhearted."

"Do not let any unwholesome talk come out of your mouths, but only what is helpful for building others up according to their needs, that it may benefit those who listen" (Ephesians 4:29 NIV).

See Also
Proverbs 18:24
Proverbs 20:6
I Peter 3:8
Romans 12:15

Chapter 9

My Neighbor, Ann: Neighbors and Choice

A neighbor may seem like an unlikely choice for a legacy, but Ann was the best neighbor of all time. (It's my journey, so I can say that.) I don't think it matters where the legacy comes from if you can say that this person has influenced you and left his or her mark on your life. I had a hard time articulating the legacy I call "choice." Again, it is a journey, so refining the description of qualities is part of the process. I believe that life is made up of choices, and when you grow into a person who makes the right choices when it counts, it's a great quality. This is a quality I want for myself and my children.

My neighbor, Ann, was very special to me. As far back as I can remember, Ann was there with her daughter, Shirley, next door to our house. Ann used to babysit Jeni and I when we got home from school until our parents came home from work.

Ann had a daughter with Down Syndrome in a time when all the experts said to institutionalize your child with disabilities. She did not. I think this speaks to her character, her strength, and love, like many others who were in her same situation. Shirley's father died when she was young, and long before I met them.

Ann had all these little things she liked, like lighthouses, collectible dolls, and most importantly her pets, which were definitely part of her family.

Ann passed away at home, very ill with cancer, the year I was married. When we knew she would not live to see me married, I brought my wedding dress home and tried it on so she could see me in the dress. She would not have been well enough to travel for the wedding even if she had lived longer. Shirley came to our wedding. Sometimes in a quiet moment, when I am holding one of my girls, I will think to myself, "I wish Ann could have met you." She loved to see "the girls," Jeni and her sisters, Lori, and Meri-K with their children. I know that we will meet again in Heaven, and Ann is one of the people I plan to search out when I get there.

I wonder if Ann ever had any idea how she impacted the lives of others. Jeni and I both went on to work with people with developmental disabilities, and for myself I know that growing up with Ann and Shirley affected me. You see, it was always normal to me. I did not think of Shirley as different.

Books and movies are full of wonderful neighbors, and plain awful neighbors. I hope that the friendly neighbors portrayed in literature aren't a thing of the past, and the inconsiderate, weird neighbors in comedies and suspense-action movies aren't representative of the present and future. At the very least I wonder if visiting with neighbors on a fairly regular basis is going out of vogue, perhaps because we are all so busy.

My parents never locked their doors when I was growing up, and we went in and out of each others' homes, playing together until dinnertime, and sometimes even dinner was spent at the neighbor's house.

Our neighbor, Ann, came over for a visit almost every day. I can still see her sitting at the kitchen table. She never stayed long, just long enough to chat about the weather or what was for dinner.

I especially think of Ann around Christmas. She loved Christmas, decorating her house, buying gifts, and lots of baking. Every year she would say, "next year I don't think I'll bake as much," but she always did. And we were always glad she did, for Ann was a fabulous baker.

We would plan a day to go over to Ann's house and exchange gifts, and Ann would bring out a beautiful platter of mouth-watering, perfectly arranged cookies. There were peanut butter balls; iced raspberry bars; frosted chocolate chip cookies (I love the audacity of frosted chocolate chip cookies); and my all-time, personal favorite, what I like to call Ann's Orange Cookies. I have made these a few times, and I am not being humble when I say they have never looked as good or tasted as amazing as Ann's.

Ann's Orange Cookies

3 ½ cups flour
1 ½ cups sugar
1 tsp baking powder
1 tsp baking soda
¾ cup shortening
¾ cup sour milk
½ tsp salt
4 tablespoons orange juice
1 tablespoon grated orange rind
3 eggs-beat
Mix by hand. Middle shelf in oven. 6 minutes, at 400.
Grease lightly.

Icing:

3 cups powdered sugar
½ of small cream cheese
3 tablespoons butter or margarine
1 tablespoon grated orange rind
Orange juice to mix to desire

That's the recipe exactly as Ann wrote it down. I have often wondered about the sour milk. I read online you can add some vinegar to milk to sour it, and that's how I get sour milk.

When I visit my parents at Christmas, I find myself still looking toward the door expecting to see Ann's face peeking in.

I loved Ann, and I am sorry I didn't get the chance to introduce my sweet girls to her, because I know she would have loved them like a grandma. When I think about what she meant to me, I know the best way to honor her is to maintain my friendship with her daughter. Nothing could have meant more to her than for me, along with my family, to cherish that relationship.

Being a great neighbor takes effort, and putting ourselves out there. I really want my children to experience visiting with neighbors, so this is another one of those legacies I need to get going on. I plan to make this the year we make and deliver some treats to the neighbors at Christmas time.

Choice

I have a distant, vague memory of Ann telling me, "when Shirley was young, they told me to put her in an institution. That is the best thing for her and you." I don't recall Ann ever talking about Shirley in any way that would suggest she was different.

I admire Ann for raising Shirley at home in a time when people knew less about Down Syndrome, and I am sure were not always the nicest. Growing up next door to someone with a developmental disability meant I didn't think anything was unusual or special about people with disabilities. It meant accepting people the way they are, for who they are. I am very grateful for this opportunity, as I think it has really impacted my life. I have had several jobs working with children and adults with developmental disabilities through the years.

Even more, I think it has instilled in me a strong emphasis on the value of human life, all life. Ann's legacy to me is to do the right thing, make the right choices when you know what the right thing to do is, regardless of others' behavior around you. No matter how cool it is to pick on the weird, strange, odd, ugly, fat, different—whatever the ugly word is here—person, it is wrong. I will always correct my children if I hear anything remotely suggesting they think they are better than someone else.

One of my favorite stories is of a woman who smuggled Jewish children out of the Warsaw ghetto during World War II. Irena Sendler kept a jar with the children's names and location where they went during the war so that those who survived could be reunited later. Sendler's father was a doctor who had been willing to treat Jewish patients at a time when many doctors would not. He left a legacy for his daughter that would result in the rescue of 2,500 children, as well as the inspiration and courage that affected those in her company. I have always had an interest in reading about World War II, which seems funny to people who know me. Noble, courageous stories like this one are very inspiring, but they also help me to appreciate what I have. More than once, when tenderly caring for one of my newborns, bathing, dressing, and feeding them, I would find myself thinking of this time period. I cannot imagine what it must have been like for a mother who cared for her precious children with so great attention and concern, to then see her own children so inhumanely treated and not be able to do anything about it. Motherhood stirs up strong feelings. I want to teach my children to make the right choices, even when it is hard, and to understand the value of all human life.

Legacy Commitment

1. Ann was a great visitor, an exceptional neighbor.
- I will step outside of my comfort zone and become a great neighbor.
- I will make a great neighborhood for my children.
2. Ann raised a child with Down Syndrome in a time when mothers were told to put their disabled children into institutions. Ann did not let others tell her what to do when she knew the right thing to do.
- I will do the right thing and value every human being no matter what others are saying or doing.
- I will steadfastly teach my children to show dignity and respect for all human beings, to live above criticizing others, to show care and concern for those in need, to do the right thing.

Thinking About Our Legacies

Are there any recipes you want to pass onto your children? Maybe you could set out to discover a recipe together that could become your family's signature dish. How can you be the best neighbor in the neighborhood, the neighbor people dream of having on their street?

I know someone who feels strongly about the therapeutic benefit of pets for older adults, but being aware of the costs of feeding and caring for animals, she donates pet food and supplies to people in need. This is a specific cause that is important to her and she does something about it.

What do you feel very strongly about? For me it is the value of human life. I can say this and talk about it, but I want to commit to demonstrating this for my girls. Take the time to think about your passionate beliefs, what you can do to show your children the strengths of your beliefs, and then start living this out.

Obviously not all of our choices are life and death choices, but it can be intriguing to look back and think about choices that have made a difference in our lives. I think it is important to share these stories with our children so they can begin to think about how small and big choices one day can impact them later.

Legacy Scripture Verses to Commit to Memory

Do not be deceived: God cannot be mocked. A man reaps what he sows. Whoever sows to please their flesh, from the flesh will reap destruction; whoever sows to please the Spirit, from the Spirit will reap eternal life. Let us not become weary in doing good, for at the proper time we will reap a harvest if we do not give up. Therefore, as we have opportunity, let us do good to all people, especially to those who belong to the family of believers. (Galatians 6:7-10 NIV)

See Also
Daniel 1:8
John 3:16

Chapter 10

Luke and Lois: Prayer and Fruit of the Spirit

I felt like I needed to create my own legacies, but I would have to say I am at the beginning of this journey. You might be able to claim legacies that you feel you already personify, or ones that you wish you did. Either way, what I think is important here, is that you put it on paper. You may choose to never share your journal with others, but its influence on your life can still be there.

There is a lot no one tells you before you embark on the parenting journey. Perhaps that's on purpose, because parents should only have to handle a little at a time. It is funny how the parenting advice changes over the years. Don't eat deli meat when you're pregnant, put babies to sleep on their backs, don't give your children juice, kids who go to preschool do better in school… There are some amazing people out there who use only cloth diapers, breastfeed until age 2, make all their own baby food, homeschool, grocery shop for the month for whatever they cannot grow in their own gardens, never go through the drive-through, bathe their kids every night, time-out every infraction, their kids don't know what candy is…I could go on , but it is making me feel bad. I will go on record here saying I love my children very much, and if I can work on the legacies I have discovered in my own background (plus a couple more I would like to add to the mix), I believe that my husband and I can raise our children for God's glory, with lots of help from the Holy Spirit and anyone He brings into our lives. I may not have the time or stomach for cloth diapers, but I have to prioritize here.

So, for my children's sake, here it is. I used disposable diapers because it was worth it to me and I trust the people who researched the financial and energy costs and determined disposable diapers were okay (this is what I desperately want to believe). I used coupons and faithfully punched in savings codes. I never bought a jar of baby food. I chopped, pureed, and froze all of their food, and oddly enough I enjoyed every minute of it. I found it strangely satisfying to prepare their food, and it wasn't bad for us to have all those fruits and vegetables around anyway. My babies slept on their backs in the room with me until I was ready to make the big move. That is all I will admit to, but if my children ever want to ask me for more details, I will happily share with them. One daughter used a pacifier, one did not, and there are benefits to both ways. I nursed one baby until one year when she was ready to be done, and one past a year. I wonder if I will remember these details correctly by the time my girls want to know? If there is one thing I have learned as a parent of young children, it is not to judge. I have a habit of saying "I'm not writing a parenting book." Now I wonder if that is still true. I think it is fun to chronicle some of the big things for my children, but I don't pretend to be a parenting expert with tips on potty training or weaning. I do admit to writing a parenting journal.

I fretted over removing the binky and baba with my oldest, and then came the question of how in the world to potty train, and really time and discipline solved all these dilemmas. I still haven't figured out how to find the time to rotate the clothes that fit/don't fit/in season/out of season, and I may never feel caught up. The laundry and dishes get done, there is pretty frequent vacuuming, and the bills get paid. A lot of other things get put on hold. That is my big parenting advice for my children. How did we do it? We didn't do a lot of things, and we decided what did need to be done. That is why I am taking all the time to write this spiritual legacy journal for my children, because I finally realize the most important thing to get done is to leave our children a spiritual legacy.

Prayer

I love reading people's stories of answered prayers. *Mama's Way* is about Thyra Ferre Bjorn's (1976) simple manner of praying about everything all the time. As I have explored the legacies left by those in my life, it has become clear very quickly I am going to need a lot of help to mimic Bjorn and become a Christ-like person, and teach my children to become

Christ-like. That is why my husband, Luke, and I are choosing prayer as our first legacy. We want our children to know us as people of prayer.

My oldest daughter likes to play church where she gets to be Mrs. Baccus, her Sunday School teacher. I was praying with her before bed one night, as I do every night, when she asked me, "are you being Mrs. Baccus?" Now with all due respect to Mrs. Baccus, I was a little put out that my daughter thought I must be pretending to be someone else because I was praying. A few days later I was reading the Bible in the morning, again like I do every morning, when my daughter asked me, "are you being Mrs. Baccus?" By now the message is clear to me. Mommy needs to read the Bible and pray regularly in full view of my children so that they know this is something everyone who lives for Christ does, not just the Sunday School teacher. There is nothing so cute as seeing my children's little hands folded together in prayer. I think God likes hearing their thanks for every animal and person they can think of, even if it is in that order.

I have read a lot of books on prayer, and my conclusion is this: It is not as hard as we make it to be. Talk to God all the time about everything. It doesn't have to be perfect, because the Holy Spirit promises to "proof" it for us. That is a pretty amazing promise. God already knows we need help talking to Him. It doesn't have to be perfectly phrased, outlined, and presented, because God can handle it. In the Old Testament, David said all kinds of things to God, and he was a man after God's own heart.

As I name prayer as a legacy that I want to define my life, and that I plan to leave my kids, I need to get serious about it. Journaling is a great way to concretely chart my progress, and a great way to connect with my husband in this endeavor. Obviously, praying over all of these legacies is an important part of prayer for me now.

The Fruit of the Spirit

I have compiled quite a list for myself. Let's review the legacies I want to pass on: mission, celebration, faith, reading, rejoice, home, simplicity, love, discipline, adventure, work, visit, friendliness, giving, kindness, friendship, neighbors, choice, prayer. What could possibly be left, right? Well as I was meditating on the lives of my loved ones, I kept thinking about two things. First, how much help I was going to need from the Holy Spirit to accomplish these things in my life, to be made into a new person, to be made like Christ. Second, I kept going back to the fruit of the Spirit I memorized as a kid, and wondering, should I just be concentrating on these instead of working through the qualities in the people in my life? I stayed with meandering through my background because I believe God directed me to. Now that I have, I choose the fruit of the Spirit for my legacy for my children. This way I am covering everything. The fruit of the Spirit are a list of qualities (fruit) that God (Spirit) promises to produce in us if we depend on Him.

But the fruit of the Spirit is love, joy, peace, patience, kindness, goodness, faithfulness, gentleness, self-control; against such things there is no law. And those who belong to Christ Jesus have crucified the flesh with its passions and desires. If we live by the Sprit, let us also keep in step with the Spirit. (Galatians 5:22-25 ESV)

When I read the fruit of the Spirit, I see these fruits in the lives of the people God brought into my life. If my children could say these things about my husband and I, then we will have done our God-given jobs.

Legacy Scripture Verses to Commit to Memory

Galatians 5:22-25

"Listen, my son, to your father's instruction and do not forsake your mother's teaching. They are a garland to grace your head and a chain to adorn your neck" (Proverbs 1:8-9 NIV).

"Enter his gates with thanksgiving and his courts with praise; give thanks to him and praise his name. For the Lord is good and his love endures forever; his faithfulness continues through all generations" (Psalm 100:4-5 NIV).

"Rejoice always, pray continually, give thanks in all circumstances; for this is God's will for you in Christ Jesus" (1 Thessalonians 5:16-18 NIV).

See Also
Psalm 34:1

Chapter 11
A Year Later

Mission and Celebration

When I started this journey, I would not have said I felt I had a mission in life. Thinking about what I consider to be my mother's calling led me to think about what might be my calling in life. Perhaps the most striking related event is that I quit my job after almost 14 years to stay home with my children. This came after much prayer and answered prayer. I started a new job working from home, teaching online. Then, my husband was offered different, better hours at work, which necessitated a change as we had worked opposite hours and avoided using day care. God provided the way for me to stay home when I could not have imagined it possible.

I had an excellent job, but I had always wanted the opportunity to stay home with my children before they started school. My oldest was 4 years old when I left my job, so this was my last chance for this experience. It seems to me many people are not happy in their jobs but stay out of desperation, fear, or hopelessness. Becoming a parent has truly enhanced how I view my heavenly Father. I know I want the best for my children, so I understand that my perfect Father feels the same way.

Sometimes we worry that we will not know God's will for our lives, that we will act out of our own motives, and never know if we made the right decision. Yet through this experience I could see that God was bringing me along, making my way clear and obvious so that I could act on His gift of answered prayer, and know to give Him the glory for it. I had prayed specifically for a certain amount of money in the bank before leaving my job, meaningful work I could do from home that would be a ministry I could serve the Lord in, and the knowledge and peace that it was the right decision. God precisely answered each of these prayers.

A year after starting this journal I can say that my life has dramatically changed. My first spiritual legacy was Mission, and my pursuit and defining of this legacy has led me on a new journey. I do not think for a minute that my past jobs or accomplishments have not been part of my mission, but in choosing this legacy, it has helped to remind me to stay on the path that God has planned for me, one that is far greater than I would have selected for myself. I believe that is because God is my Father and wants the best for me, so that even when I pray for what seems outrageous, I know that He can do it. There are things my children may want, but I understand that they might not be ready for something, or that it might not be the right thing for them. God in His perfect wisdom provides for us at the right time what we need (Psalm 145:14-16).

I pray that in the next year I will have defined my mission even more, so that like my mother's calling, I will be able to clearly state what my gift is and how I will use it to help people. I want to model this type of purposeful living for my children, so that they will grow toward finding and living out their missions.

I may find that it was just an excuse, but at this point I believe that so much of my life was tied up in my job, that I did not have enough time and energy to devote to other avenues. I felt overwhelmed by my desire to be a good teacher and role model for my children, and be excellent in my job. I found that I could not be excellent at both. So now I am hoping that I will be able to devote myself more to learning and living these spiritual legacies. Even something as fun and seemingly simple as Celebration, is made so much easier without two full-time jobs (counting my career and family). I confess I did not send out Christmas cards this year, I did not make my girls' birthday cakes (my mother-in-law is amazing at this), and in the spirit of Alice in Wonderland, there were no Happy Un-birthdays this year. All said though, I would say this mission of Celebration may already be a strength of mine. When I look ahead, my prayer for Celebration is that I focus on decorating and celebrating big and little things in ways that do not mean simply spending a lot of money on stuff we do not need, and involving fewer chocolate chip cookies and cheese puffs (don't tell my kids I said that part).

Faith and Reading

I cannot say that I have made much if any progress in the legacy of faith over the past year. I recognize it as an excuse, but I cannot stress enough how busy and overwhelmed I felt working full time and raising children. If this journey has pointed nothing else out to me, it has certainly shown me that I was too busy with less important things, and that my life needed an overhaul. Being tired and busy from work was a ready excuse. I have simplified my life in many ways this past year.

There are some techniques I implemented this year as a result of this journey. I wrote out all of the Scripture verses I wanted to memorize on colored index cards. Unfortunately, this turned out to be a bad idea with young children drawn to the pretty colored cards. So, I guess I will need to rewrite the verses on white cards. I carried the cards around in my purse for a while, and I even bought a small Bible that would fit in my purse to have with me. I found I was not using either, to be honest. Most people I know have the Bible on their phone, but I guess I am too old fashioned for this. I framed the fruit of the Spirit and placed it where I will see it each time I leave the bedroom (Galatians 5:22-23). A reminder to rejoice in each day greets me when I get out of the shower in the morning (Psalm 118:24).

My New Year's resolutions are now replaced by my prayers for the year, and I have faith God will answer as He has so wonderfully in this past year. I have more consistently and continuously given my attention to matters of faith this year. I bought a children's devotional book to read with my family. It doesn't even take five minutes, which is a good thing with toddlers. Something as simple as praying as a family before meals takes discipline to consistently do. I picture my faith spreading out and covering our lives more, instead of my faith growing in a vertical way.

Reading continues to be a big part of my life, my husband's, and now our children's lives. This is another one of those legacies that is a strength for me. I always need to remind myself to be selective in choosing what to read, and when to read. I am looking forward to reading my favorite children's books together with my girls. One idea for implementing this legacy is to find books to read that address each of my spiritual legacies.

Home and Rejoice

A year ago I asked for a book on container gardening for Christmas, which while I enjoyed reading, I never put into practice. Reading this legacy again reminds me of my goal to do more gardening with my girls. We have been busy working together outdoors, and now I wonder why I thought a house with a big yard was such a great idea. Needless to say, not working a full-time job outside of the home will make this legacy far more attainable.

It is quickly becoming obvious to me that I need to pay more attention to the spiritual legacies I spent so much time planning. It strikes me that keeping a nice home and making each day special may sound simplistic and self-serving, but it is more involved than that to me. I feel like our culture puts value in how we take care of ourselves, and in how we fill and decorate our homes, but there are unglamorous chores and uninspired days as well. I like these Home and Rejoice legacies because they require daily attention. I have the opportunity to practice these legacies almost continuously throughout the day. I do not even know where to start when it comes to organizing the home, but let's just say it needs more attention.

Simplicity and Love

I still have too much stuff. I don't know where it is all coming from. Is someone coming into my house when I am not there and stuffing closets, toy boxes, and cupboards? Of course not. I guess it must be ours. I continue to donate regularly, so at least I know some things are leaving the house. It has been a cold winter so far, and my youngest is not as fond of leaving the house as the rest of us, so that has helped to curb the spending. Two kids yelling and running around Target helps to keep the shopping trips short and quick.

I recently watched a documentary on diamond mining in Africa, and diamonds seemed silly by the end of it. All that money, time, and effort exhausted on pulling stones from the ground in a world with much bigger needs. I no longer feel the need for diamond earrings. Hopefully, the thought lasts. I think it is a good idea to watch these documentaries, keep in touch with what is happening in the bigger world, so that I get a better idea of what it is I really need. It is so much easier to see other people's extravagances. In the interest of this legacy, I am committing to learning more about other's needs, focusing less on mine. This will also help to increase my love for others.

Discipline and Adventure

This legacy of discipline pulled together several of the legacies for me. My first thought in the area of discipline was for weight loss. I have tried many weight loss programs in my life. Since my youngest daughter is three now, it seems unreasonable to keep blaming her for the extra weight. Year after year I pray for weight loss, while contemplating how ridiculous it is that this should be my foremost goal every year.

I suppose in a way, discipline represents a double legacy for me, since it is my sister's legacy, and a fruit of the Spirit. I find myself praying for this fruit daily, begging really. Of course, I need discipline in far more than just eating and exercising. This is where the legacy of discipline pulled in other fruits of the Spirit for me. Gentleness, patience, and kindness have lined up for their turn. I need discipline in how I interact with my children, and this to me means the above fruits in abundance. Thankfully, the Holy Spirit is happy to remind me each time I make a bad choice in how I speak. This has a lot to do with the various kinds of messes that small children make, and I am learning gentleness, patience, and kindness at their hands. I like to read the Gospels and try to soak up the kindness shown by Jesus. It has occurred to me that discipline is about energy. I can use my energy to be angry, or I can use my energy to remain calm. When I look at it like this, it takes out the emotional piece, and pushes me to think rationally about the choices I make.

Then came discipline in the work that needs to be done. I had become rigid about when and how I needed to do things. I have to get my exercise in the morning. I cannot do work in the evening. I may not be able to, but the Spirit reminded me that I have God's power to work with, and that is a different matter altogether. The kind of power that created the universe is enough for me to walk 30 minutes on the treadmill in the afternoon, even though I would prefer to do it in the morning. I had to change my mindset about what was possible and necessary. I found out it is possible to grade papers in the evening, with God's power and the Spirit's discipline.

Another big need for discipline is in the area of spending, which relates back to my legacy of simplicity. Paying the bills feels a little like Jesus dividing the loaves of bread and fishes, because God always takes care of us. Expenses that are unexpected to me, are not to Him. Having seen God continue to supply our needs in the past year, and answer financial goals, like paying for a minivan, I am praying for another big financial goal this year. Whenever I pray about money, I talk honestly with God about the help I need to rely on Him for security, reputation, and meaning in life, to keep my motives pure and in line with what He has planned for me. I am reading Jeremiah on the treadmill this week, and I have come across some gems. While buying and worshipping idols is not in my culture, I can see how money can be an idol. People looked to their idols for security and identity. God's conversation with Jeremiah is fascinating. I particularly like how He compares idols to a "scarecrow in a melon patch," unable to speak or walk, needing to be carried (Jer. 10:5 NIV). In Jeremiah 10:23, Jeremiah states, "I know, O Lord, that a man's life is not his own; it is not for man to direct his steps" (NIV). This is reassuring to me, as I would much rather have God direct my steps than me. I plan to continue reading Jeremiah with a view of money as an idol, and a view of God as the all-powerful Creator who said, "Should you not tremble in my presence?" (Jer. 5:22 NIV).

I have been surprised to find that discipline is related to so many other legacies, as I have spent most of my life considering it in the sole context of a desire to lose weight. It is much bigger of course. Now I see discipline in terms of how I live as a person who wants to be like Christ. I must become disciplined in the fruits of the Spirit and in prayer, and in all of these legacies I choose to live and pass on to my children. Every single day is a possibility to grow more in discipline, and this continues to be one of my greatest needs.

I suppose discipline is an adventure. Certainly leaving a secure job after 14 years qualifies as an adventure, so I think it is safe to say I have made some progress in this legacy in the past year. It has been about two months since I started my new life, at my home with my children, and not a day goes by that I do not ponder how blessed and happy I am. Don't get me wrong, there are plenty of frustrating, messy moments with kids and a house, but I recognize it for the incredible blessing that it is. Then I feel a little guilty for being so amazed, when this is what I prayed and asked God for, and He answered my prayer, so shouldn't the results be obvious to me? Going back to Jer. 10:23, I am so glad to be on God's path for my life, and I have no doubt this will be an adventure.

I am not sure it is necessary to seek adventure when you have kids, because this happens naturally, but I have been busy searching out big and little adventures for the family. We have been very busy having fun and making memories in the last couple of months since I have been home. Of course, adventure happened when I worked outside the home too, but it is not as frantic now. I think kids naturally see each day as an adventure, and they expect big things out of every day. I read Psalm 118:24 on my wall every morning when I get out of the shower. "This is the day which the Lord hath made; we will rejoice and be glad in it" (KJV). This makes me think about how to make the day special, and reminds me how I want to live in the fruit of the Spirit.

Work and Visit

I love working from home. I was never good at having a lot of bosses. I am not saying that is right, I am just admitting it. My new boss? Jesus. I have Col. 3:23-24 on my desk. "Whatever you do, work at it with all your heart, as working for the Lord, not for men, since you know that you will receive an inheritance from the Lord as your reward. It is the Lord Christ you are serving" (NIV). It helps that I know this new life is a gift from God, an answered prayer. I have this in mind every day as I strive to do my best for my family, and in my new job.

I have to be on guard to not just work hard to get the work done, but to take the time to do it to the best of my ability, and with frequent prayer, so that I am not doing it alone. As a counseling professor for a Christian university, I am investing in people's lives and in the people they will serve in the future. Again, discipline is involved with this legacy. And again, I am amazed at how much my life has changed in the past year.

There is a lot of work involved in having a family. I know, an obvious statement. One of the most significant concepts I have come across that has helped me as a parent, is found in Gary Chapman's *The 5 Love Languages*. The idea that doing things for my children is a way that I can show my love to them, has been very important to me, and instrumental in changing my entire mindset. I want to complain and vent about how much I have to do, the house is always messy, no one cleans up after themselves, and how changing your clothes all day long makes more laundry for me, and I won't go on and on here, but you get the point. When I think about serving my family as a way of showing my love for them, this makes all the difference for me. I am not saying I have made a full recovery yet, but I try to keep it in mind when I am serving. I also keep in mind how easy it is to throw clothes in a machine, wait 45 minutes, and throw them in another machine.

The picture of Jesus washing His disciples' feet in John 13 is a vivid reminder to me to serve others, and in particular, my family. I can never get over the humility of Jesus. Certainly, if I am to become like Him, I need to be a servant, and I believe this starts at home. Needless to say, He did not complain while he washed big, dirty men's feet. There is humility in any work we do, as everyone has people to answer to, no matter how important your title.

I like to visit with the people I like to visit with, so if there is one thing in this area I need to make some progress in, it is to widen my visiting. I don't know if you would exactly call them visits, but Jesus did some interesting visiting. There are so many beautiful pictures of Jesus taking His time with people from all walks of life. I am sure there is a message in here for me. If I do not take the time and effort, not to mention stepping outside my comfort zone, to be with others, how will I be Christ for the world? I have to admit, I don't love this one. I like sitting alone reading a book, and there is merit in that for sure, but it is not always the best use of my time. Close family, extended family, friends, neighbors, church family, strangers...there are a lot of people to pay attention to. Once I reminded myself of this legacy, I made some phone calls and visited with family and friends.

Friendliness and Giving

From visiting to friendliness, I am not the most outgoing of people. In fact, it feels fake sometimes, but I still attempt to make the effort. I cannot think of much I have done in the past year to reinforce this legacy. I'm a work in progress.

I just realized when I did my taxes that I managed to do less charitable giving last year compared to the previous year, though we made more money. That's not good. It's a new year now, and we are off to a good start. To be honest, I have to pray a lot about tithing and giving in general. I wish I could say it comes easy, but I can be a miser. I think nothing of buying and giving in some areas, but then pinch pennies in the next area, with no rhyme or reason to it.

I have to think about money as God's provision to us. As a parent, I want the best for my children, but I also understand it is not best for them to have everything. God is my Father and has always provided us with what we need. Discipline is critical again with this legacy. I think I will begin to thank God every time we spend money. I will thank Him for the money to put gas in the vehicles, something I take for granted now. I will thank Him for the money to pay the bills. I hope this step, which may seem obvious to others, but will be new to me, will help me to be more conscious of money as God's provision for us. I also think it will cause me to be more aware of how I am spending money, as it could be awkward to thank God for the money to buy a bunch of stuff at Target that we do not need. It is my hope that the constant reminder that God provides for us, that this is His money, will make giving easier. My verse I use for support is Phil. 4:19, "and my God will meet all your needs according to His glorious riches in Christ Jesus" (NIV). Paul said this to the church that financially supported him.

I feel better coming up with a plan. So this legacy of giving is tied to discipline and prayer for me. I am finding that my long list of legacies are far more related than I first realized. The other surprise has been a better understanding of my own dissertation written years ago. I wrote about the power of writing in therapy, and I am experiencing it firsthand now, in a way I did not fully understand before. The combination of journaling about my chosen legacies, and absorbing God's Word are transforming me. I am daily finding the promise of 2 Tim. 3:16-17 to be true: "All Scripture is God-breathed and is useful for teaching, rebuking, correcting and training in righteousness, so that the man of God may be thoroughly equipped for every good work" (NIV). I am afraid the post-it notes are starting to accumulate around me. Today I added post-it notes with Phil. 4:19 to the binder I use to coordinate paying the household bills, and to my wallet. It is not that I worry about having enough money, or even that I want more money, it is that I have a hard time giving, and too easy of a time spending.

Kindness and Friendship

I continue to emphasize kindness with my girls, and to keep the comments on outward appearance at least even with comments on kind actions. I think of kindness as a state of being. It is especially important to me to be thought of as kind, and for my girls to be kind. I cannot explain why this is so much easier for me than discipline in general.

Again discipline rears its ugly head, for it takes discipline to maintain friendships in our fast paced, busy world. I don't like the progress I haven't made in the past year in this area. I am not the most outgoing person, and I have never been one for a crowd, so I can't say as I have a long list of friends. That should make it easier, right? So, in the interest of renewing this legacy, I have made a list of four friends I plan to cherish in the upcoming year. I like my behavioral techniques, so I made a list, and now I am going to plan to maintain monthly contact. That might not sound like a lot, but you have to start somewhere. Of course, my childhood friend Jenniffer is on the list. One friend from high school, one from college, and one local friend round out the list.

Neighbors and Choice

As it happens, my girls played in our neighbor's dirt a couple of nights ago. I was in the zone catching up on a couple years' worth of gardening (by which I mean pulling weeds), and not paying enough attention to my girls who were happily making a mess next door. I looked up, and my neighbor was looking out his window at them. I was scared. Was he mad? Was he thinking, "oh, the cute little angels"? I don't know, but I put an end to their raking and shoveling (with a snow shovel, I might add) at once. The next day we made chocolate chip cookies and delivered them with an apology. Turns out, they weren't mad. They were thinking they were cute and having fun. And, our neighbor has diabetes, so cookies were not a great idea. But, I did it. I reached out to a neighbor. We also managed to invite other neighbors with kids to a birthday party this year, so I suppose we are making some minimal progress in this area, enough to avoid feeling dejected. Still, there is much to do here. I don't know if I am ready to tackle a neighborhood picnic, but the fact that I would even think about it, I believe to be a step in the right direction. I'm so easy on myself.

I think I might still be making far more bad choices than good choices, so here is another area for great improvement to be made. I actually forgot about this legacy, so just reading about it again, I hope will spark more effort on my part.

Prayer and Fruit of the Spirit

A year later, I cannot say that I am praying more. I have definitely seen the results of prayer all around me throughout my life, and specifically in the past year. I am beginning to think everything is related to discipline. My most significant conclusion is that my family is my mission. I am serving Christ right here and now, and my prayer life needs to begin. I pray for the Holy Spirit to dwell in me and give me the fruit of the Spirit, but every single day I fail in many ways to exhibit discipline in how I speak with my children, how I spend money, and most importantly, how I do not spend time with God. Every day slips by with no more progress on prayer or the fruit of the Spirit.

The dilemma is how to carry these goals in front of me every day. How do I keep this on my mind, working toward a life marked by prayer and the fruit of the Spirit? I act like there will be some magic idea or special prayer that will transform me. I have tried all kinds of behavioral techniques out on myself, short of tattooing the fruit of the Spirit on my arm. If I have learned anything in the last year, it is that there are no short cuts.

Growing up, my parents had a sign over the back door that said, "You are now entering the mission field." That always perplexed me as a child, to see a sign about entering something different on the other side of the door. Later, I came to understand the meaning behind it, but now as an adult, I wonder if it is entirely correct. Viewing my home as my mission field is a powerful concept for me. The budget I follow is different when I view this as a mission. The interactions I have, and the goals I set are different.

This is the message I have from God as I think back over these legacies. I am already a missionary. This is my mission field. As a missionary I need to pray and guide others in the same spiritual disciplines that I am carrying out. I could see this in others, but until I realized that I am a missionary right now, I was acting just like anyone else in the world. I may not be Mother Teresa in Calcutta but I am God's chosen missionary right here, right now for His purpose. I have been reading about people I admire, thinking about the disparity between my life and theirs, and not realizing I can get to work right now.

My life as a missionary gives me the motivation for discipline that I need. God is telling me how important my role is right now. I can work on these legacies, because this is my job now. It is my mission. I am serving God full time. I did not see it before now.

Conclusion

Proverbs 1:8-9 states, "Hear, my son, your father's instruction, and forsake not your mother's teaching, for they are a graceful garland for your head and pendants for your neck" (ESV).

When I first embarked on this journey, I had no idea the wealth of legacies I would uncover when I sat down again and again to really think about the people in my life who have helped shape me. I quickly found I have a lot of work to do, if I am serious about passing these 20 legacies onto my children. I am glad I don't have to do it alone. While I have spoken in the first person throughout this journey, I am blessed to be on this journey with a wonderful, patient husband. Together, we can begin to consciously teach our children values.

It is my hope that you have been encouraged to examine your background and choose the life lessons you want to pass on to your children. Over and over as I was writing, the word choice kept coming back to me. I have a choice to live with these character traits. I make choices every day all day long how to live my life and how to teach my children. With all these choices to make, I think a lesson plan is a good idea.

The model I hoped to convey in this book is to first explore your memories of the people in your life, and then, with God's help and direction, decide on one or two legacies for each person. It just happened that I came up with two legacies per person, but of course that may vary for you. I like things nice and neat, so once I had a pattern I stuck with it. Once I had chosen legacies, I worked on getting each legacy down to one word. Again, this is not a necessary step, but I think it is easier to bring to mind individual words and really mull them over.

I found this especially beneficial when I explored what faith and love, words we throw around, really mean to me. Next, I wrote a simple statement of commitment, thinking about how I would embrace this legacy in my life. After my commitment, it was a statement about how I would pass this legacy onto my children.

This has been a great exercise, but the real challenge is how to make this come alive. Writing out and memorizing Bible verses that support these legacies has been helpful. I also bought some nice paper, printed out the most significant Bible verses, matted and framed these, and put them somewhere special as a constant reminder. I printed all of my legacies on one page and framed it on my desk. For some unknown reason, and perhaps an ironic one, my girls keep walking off with it. They are using it as a tray. Sometimes there is something tangible you can do in the moment to show your commitment to a legacy, such as making and delivering treats to the neighbors at Christmas time (yes, I really did do this). I tried to choose a legacy each month to concentrate on, but I forgot this plan within a few months. Maybe one a year would be better?

Sharing these legacies with my husband and others means accountability. Once others know I am committed to working on these character traits, I want to live up to the standards, I want to become the person I wrote about in these pages. You don't need to be married with children to explore your legacies. I wish I had started thinking about legacies years ago before I was married, before children. I do think it is important to find someone you trust to share your legacies with. Even if you do not share with another person, write it down, make a declaration for yourself.

I am pleased that I have finally begun a journal I can pass onto my children. My next step is to grow these legacies. Maybe one day I can help my girls write their own spiritual legacy journals.

Do not think for a minute that I exemplify these 20 legacies. This is the project of my life now…to live these legacies and pass them onto my children. My personal interpretation of the theme of *Daniel Deronda* by Charles Dickens is to live your life so that others around you are better off for having known you. We can say we want to be Christ-like, but until we stop and think about this and decide what this means, how can we make a plan for working toward Christlikeness? How can we tackle something as big as leaving a spiritual legacy for our children without a game plan?

Choose your legacies, commit to living those legacies, and plan to pass those legacies onto your children and others you might be influencing right now.

About the Author

Lois Mayo is an adjunct online professor working from home in upstate New York. She lives with her husband, two daughters, and two cats. Lois has worked in various counseling and support jobs, and believes in the therapeutic nature of reading and writing. She enjoys planning and carrying out fun activities and trips with her family, like baking, reading, playing school, and the next vacation.

www.ingramcontent.com/pod-product-compliance
Lightning Source LLC
Chambersburg PA
CBHW022156080426
42734CB00006B/457